FOOTPRINTS IN SAND : WALKING THROUGH TIME

BY
BARRY C. DORN

Copyright © 2024 Barry C. Dorn

All rights reserved.

No portion of this book may be reproduced in any form without written permission from the publisher or author except as permitted by U.S. copyright law

This book will be dedicated to Andrew Rolnick. " My grandson, a student at Wake Forest, who has done a phenomenal job organizing the entire work. "

TABLE OF CONTENTS

A CHANGE OF SEASON 2

A DAY IN AFRICA 4

A JOURNEY OF THE MIND 6

A MEASURE OF TIME 8

A SUMMER MOMENT 10

A TROUBLED TIME 13

ACCIDENTS ARE NOT ALL BAD 14

AFRICA'S FATE 17

ALONE IN MY WORLD 19

CHAPTR THREE 21

COMPASSION 24

DESPAIR II 25

DESPAIR 27

THE ESSENCE OF LIFE 29

FATE 31

FOUNDATIONS 33

HAPPINESS OR DESPAIR 36

HUMAN NATURE 38

Hi Ho Hi Ho 40

I HAVE WALKED 42

I MISS THE STREAM 44

INDECISION AND PAIN	47
LEARNING	48
Life	49
LIFE'S MOMENTS	51
LIVE AS A CHILD	54
LONELINESS	56
MY AWAKENING	59
MY MORNING	60
OJO CALIENTE I	61
OJO CALIENTE II	63
OLD CAPE COD	65
OPENING THE DOOR	67
OUT OF AFRICA	68
SANDIA MOUNTAINS	71
SO WHAT	73
THE CHAMBERS OF MY MIND	75
THE DARKNESS	77
THE END	79
THE ENDLESS JOURNEY	81
THE GARDEN	83
THE HARDEST CLIMB	85
THE JOY OF LONELINESS	87

THE LONG WALK 90

THE RELEASE OF LOVE 92

THE SAILOR'S LAMENT 94

THE SCULPTOR 96

THE SOUNDS OF LOVE 98

THE ULTIMATE BLOW 100

THE WINTER CHILL 102

THE WORDS OF LOVE 104

THE YAMMA-YAMMA MACHINE 106

TODAY 108

TORMENT 110

UNTITLED 112

WHEN WILL I AWAKEN 114

WHO WILL BE THE FIRST TO DIE 116

WRITER'S CRAMP 117

A BIRTHDAY THOUGHT 118

MY LOVE 119

A BIRTHDAY THOUGHT 121

A LIFE WELL LIVED 123

A LIFE WELL LIVED 2 124

FISHING 125

GALVESTON 127

LITTLE RED SCHOOLHOUSE 128

SUNDAY IN THE PARK 130

THE COLONEL 133

THE HUNTER 134

THE PASSING 136

THE POND...137

THE RAIN..139

VALENTINES DAY 2024..141

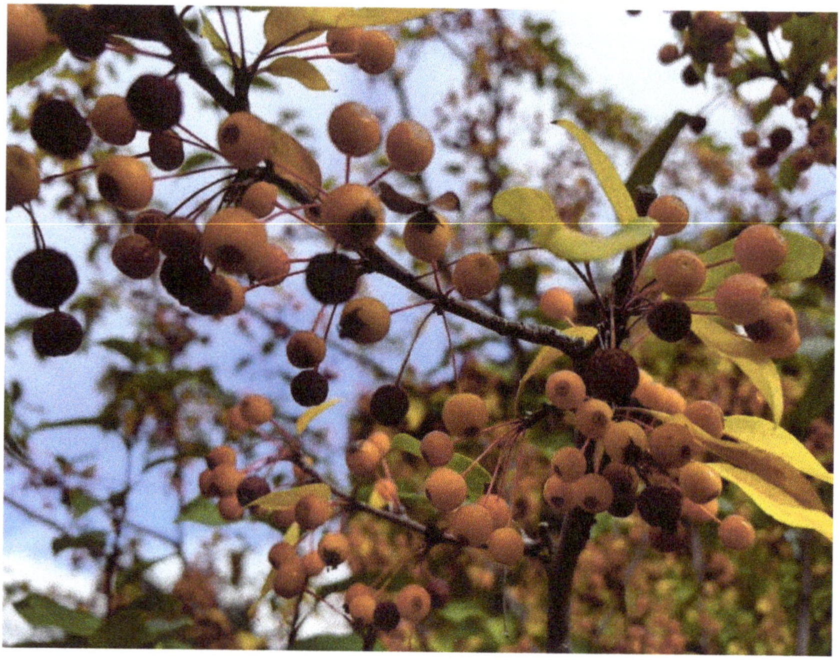

A CHANGE OF SEASON

I can feel the gentle bite in the air
The leaves flutter in the wind and cover the cool earth
And I see a rebirth and not a death
I see a crackling fire, the gentle light flickering off your face

I am at peace in a place of warmth and comfort
I reach out and, in the silence, I touch your hand
You smile and the gentle light casts a glow over us
Two people oh, so connected, in every way

Two hearts beating as one, awaiting the first falling of snow
To cover our secret garden, painting the reds and greens with a soft blush of white
The colors dance and sparkle in the flickering light

The change in the world heralds a new closeness
An intertwining of emotions which serve to energize

Instead of mourning the change of a season
We celebrate a period of closeness and mutual satisfaction

We move closer, gathering our warmth from the other
Recognizing that together we are much more than one person alone could ever be

The sum of two being so much more powerful than the individual

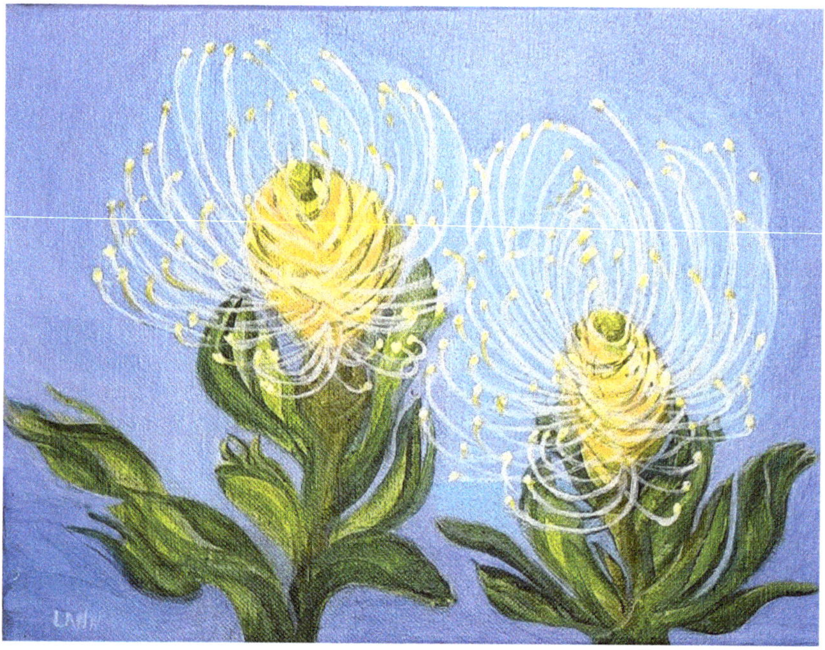

A DAY IN AFRICA

Yellow, green, purple and black dart across the sky
The tall grass waves in the warm sweet air
And the world is quiet in a gentle sort of way

A large grey shadow enters into view followed by the soft, firm plodding of the herd
They pull the tall grass up in clumps and mow down the Tangari lawn
A baby rolls over in a mud hole, blowing water from his trunk and splashing about
His mother nudges him from the mud hole and moves him to the center of the herd
Just as quietly as they appeared, they wander off into the Acacia grove

As they move off into the distance, a long spotted neck can be seen high in the Acacia
Its tiny ears wiggle and two small birds fly from atop their lofty perch
Soon others appear and the canopy of trees are expertly trimmed by their long, undulating necks
They move with ease and grace until startled and then disappear in a gallop into the vegetation

The afternoon sun beats down and warms our faces as we move about
We sit to rest and watch as the sun makes its way to the horizon
Then in a last blast of brilliance, the sun dives below the horizon
The dusk deepens to night and once again the symphony of the night creatures begin

Some rest and retire, others exit their habitat to feed
Another day on the Serengeti. From birth to death
From light to dark. The world is in balance

A JOURNEY OF THE MIND

The time of trial has arrived
It came with a bang, not the soft entrance I had planned
It has affected all our lives
The feelings of love, remorse, anxiety, and pain
Mix together in the cauldron of the mind
They appear, disappear, reappear, and continuously repeat the cycle

They are inescapable
There are brief moments when the thoughts are clear and controlled
And there are others when everything blends in an amalgam of chaos
That overcomes rational thought and caries one to a dark place
A dark place that gives only pain and never respite
A place that takes control of all other thoughts
Especially the ones of joy and tenderness

How is one to survive the constant onslaught of the wandering mind?
It is certainly not by control
It is certainly not by the force of will
It is only by the nonjudgmental acceptance of what is

If one has a mind, it will wander
The attempt to control it is fruitless and exhausting
Only acceptance, recognition, and letting go will suffice

Man wants to control
To direct the thought process down a comfortable path
This cannot be and will never be
Only the acceptance of what is will set one free

This is an arduous and painful journey
Yet even the longest journeys are defined by their ending

The question is simple
Can man endure?

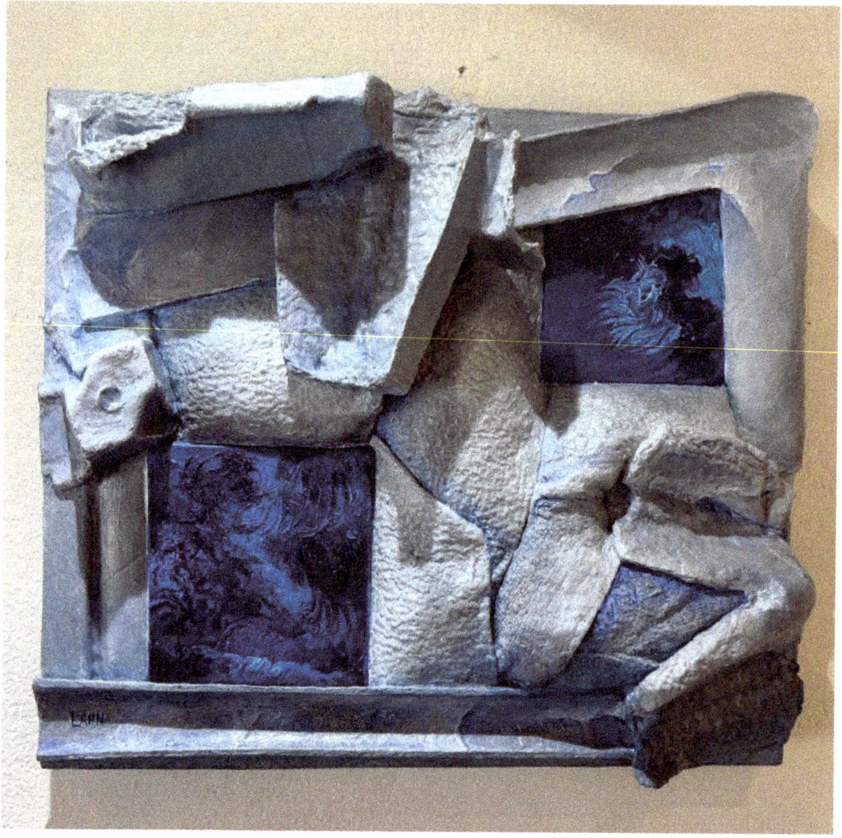

A MEASURE OF TIME

A moment comes and goes
Like an electron hurtling through time and space

The moments build
They come together
They take form
Another year forms, comes, and goes

A massive collection of moments
Some pleasurable, some distasteful
Yet equally present
The moments are little packets of time
They are equally present
But are we?

Do we absorb and experience them
Or do they pass through, unobserved?

Take time. Stop. Seize the moment
In reality that is all we have
This is a moment. I can see it, can you?

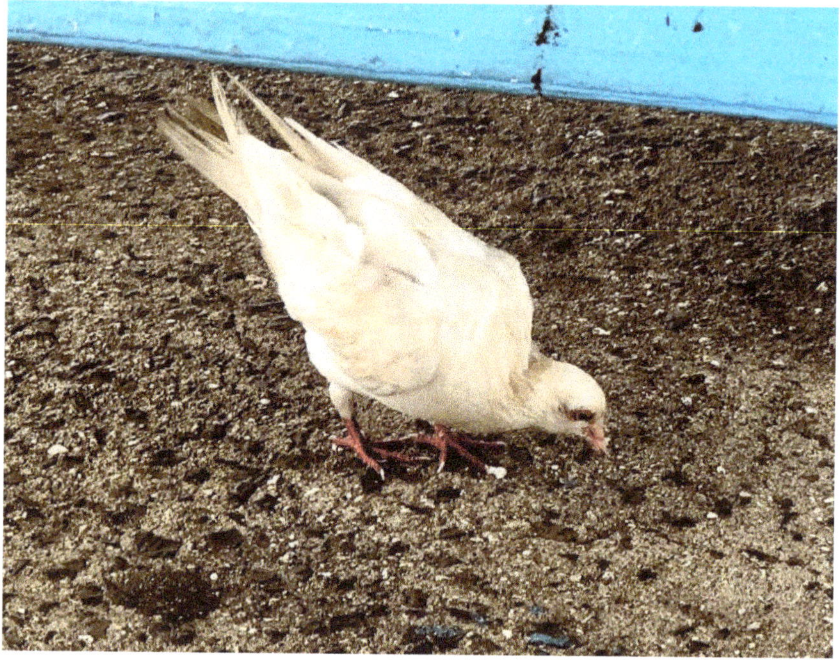

A SUMMER MOMENT

On gentle wings the bird floats to the earth
catching he corner of my eye

His white feathers slash across the deep green carpet

It stands as a statue
never moving, always ready

I turn my head to look
in a flash, it leaves the earth

Ever so softly and ever so sure

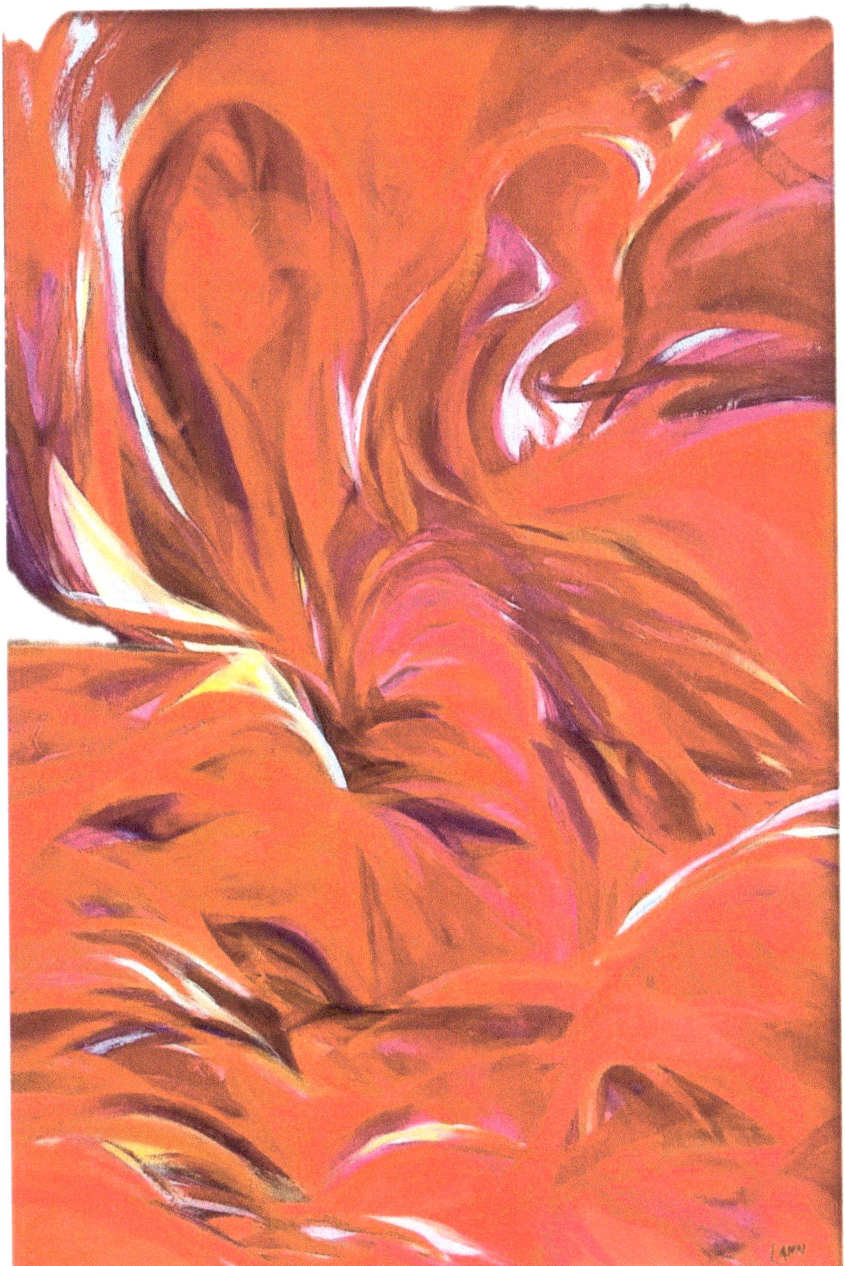

A TROUBLED TIME

My thoughts are a jumble of disconnected feelings and torments
I can't seem to focus
Everything is rushing about like rip currents in the tide

And always they return to you
I see your face everywhere, and I see your touch in everything I touch
I cannot escape it
I guess I don't want to escape it.

I see you with another man
And I cannot control my agitation
Any touch of your skin is an onslaught to my soul
Your smile to him, an invitation
That I want to snatch away

I need your presence in my life
I need you to hear my voice
To touch my hand
To excite my heart

I am adrift
I can see the shore
And yet cannot navigate it

I can see your image
But it fades over time
Am I losing you forever?

ACCIDENTS ARE NOT ALL BAD

The patient lay amongst the crumpled sheets looking pale against the white background
The IV tubes were twisted and the patient felt dry and restless
The surgery was just over 36 hours ago, and he still could not make sense of time
It all blended together in an amalgam of day and night with constant interruptions

His life had changed in the flash of an instant
He had been walking through the snow, plodding under the weight of his Christmas gifts
The snow smacked against his face, sometimes blinding him momentarily
He thought the light was green as he started to cross

The next recollection was the feeling of intense cold and pain
He was lying in the street and the paramedics were talking to him
"What is your name? Do you have any allergies? Are you on medication?"
Initially he was confused, and then the pain in his legs brought him to reality

He was placed on a litter, his packages, all disassembled, were piled on him
He heard the sound of the siren, felt cold and drifted off to a deep sleep

His next recollection was the intense pain in his right leg
And a young female nurse talking to him
He had no recollection of who he was or what had happened
And the initial pain in the leg was insignificant to the mounting pain in his head

Thoughts of who he was and what happened played over and over on the tape in his head
He was a non-person. A man without a past and an uncertain

future

His next visitor was an attractive woman in her late fifties
She was happy to see him and leaned over to kiss him
Who was this person, and why was she kissing him?
He drew back and could see the shocked look on her face
She started to cry, and he was confused. He felt her discomfort but wasn't sorry

She fled the room, looking for the nurse
He sat up, felt dizzy, and moved his painful leg
What had happened to his life and why was it suddenly gone?
He struggled to get up and pulled his IV pole with him

He walked to the window and looked out at the fresh snow
Where was he and what was he doing here Only the pain in his leg and head were real

For weeks he lay in this confused state, and the woman kept coming back
She spoke to him like she knew him, she said she was his wife, told him stories about his life

Gradually, he began to paint the picture of a life he had lived
It didn't sound like something he could like, nor did it excite him

They told him he would be discharged to the woman's care in the morning
That night he got up, dressed into the clothes in his closet, and walked out the door
Where was he going and what was he going to do? He wasn't sure

But he was certain of two things
He didn't relish the old life and he wanted more
He had been reborn and would start anew
Accidentally, he had been reborn
This was his Christmas present

AFRICA'S FATE

I sit on the veranda of my Safari lodge; gentle breezes tickle the flowers in my garden
The song birds sing and dart back and forth through the manicured vegetation
The air smells fresh and clean. The sounds of only the natural world surround me
All around me I can control. Things happen as I wish them to happen
Tomorrow I will arise and enter another world

My Land Rover will take me over the highway and into the hard packed dirt of the Serengeti
It is a world in which I am a visitor. I have no control
This is a world that belongs to nature. To the animals which make it home
I pass through it, a visitor, protected by the metal of my vehicle and the canvas and campfire of my campsite
I observe and I am observed. Both parties stare back at wonder of the other

This is a world now "protected" by man
But this will change
When we see it as a reservoir of resources rather than something to preserve and cherish
When and who will decide to change it, to tame it, to make it answer to our will?
When will the Safari lodge be ever present and the spectacular Serengeti just another zoo?
I hope I fail to see it.

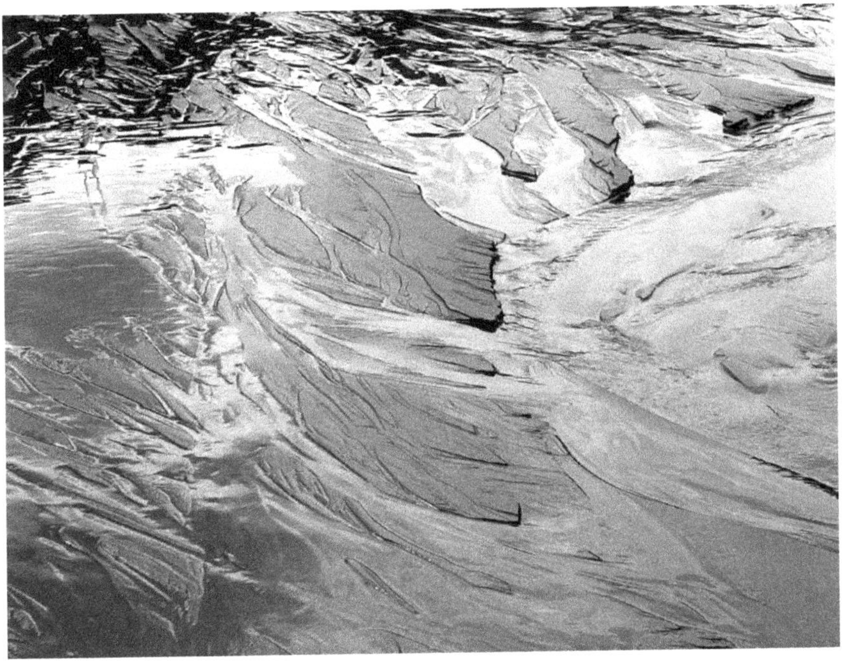

ALONE IN MY WORLD

I am surrounded by family and friends
People who care very much about me
And yet I am very alone
Because you are not with me.

You are always in my thoughts
I cannot eliminate your presence
Probably because I don't want to
I want us to be together

I want to share life with you
I want to share every moment with you
I want to be in your life
And you to be in mine

I am so lonely that I hurt
And I feel for you
Because I know you are suffering
You too are alone in your crowd

We must make time for each other
We need to create a special space
A space in which we can thrive…and survive
The crowd around us

We must learn to carve out moments of joy
Steal them from our usual humdrum lives
Moments that will keep us alive
Moments that will allow us to live
In a world which does not recognize us

Although alone in the world
We will always be together

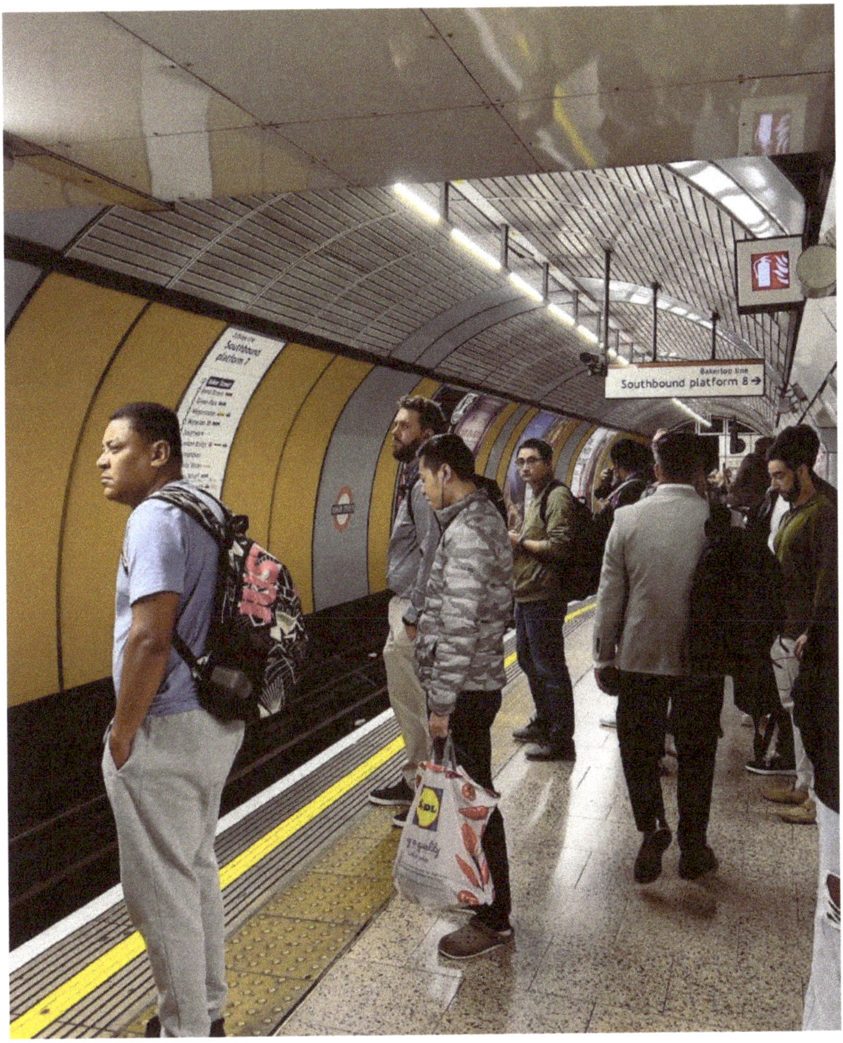
Bakerloo line
Southbound platform 8 →

CHAPTR THREE

As I count the days past and picture the days ahead
I realize the book is coming to an end

What can I hope for? What can I have?
Will it be deferred gratification of past years?
Will my children become wealthy?
Will they remember what I have given?

Or will it be a time of satisfaction
Appreciating the moment
Never looking ahead
But finally looking at now

Building things I need
Not deferring
Not thinking of others
Finally getting off the train
Enjoying the present station and only getting on again
Only if I truly want to

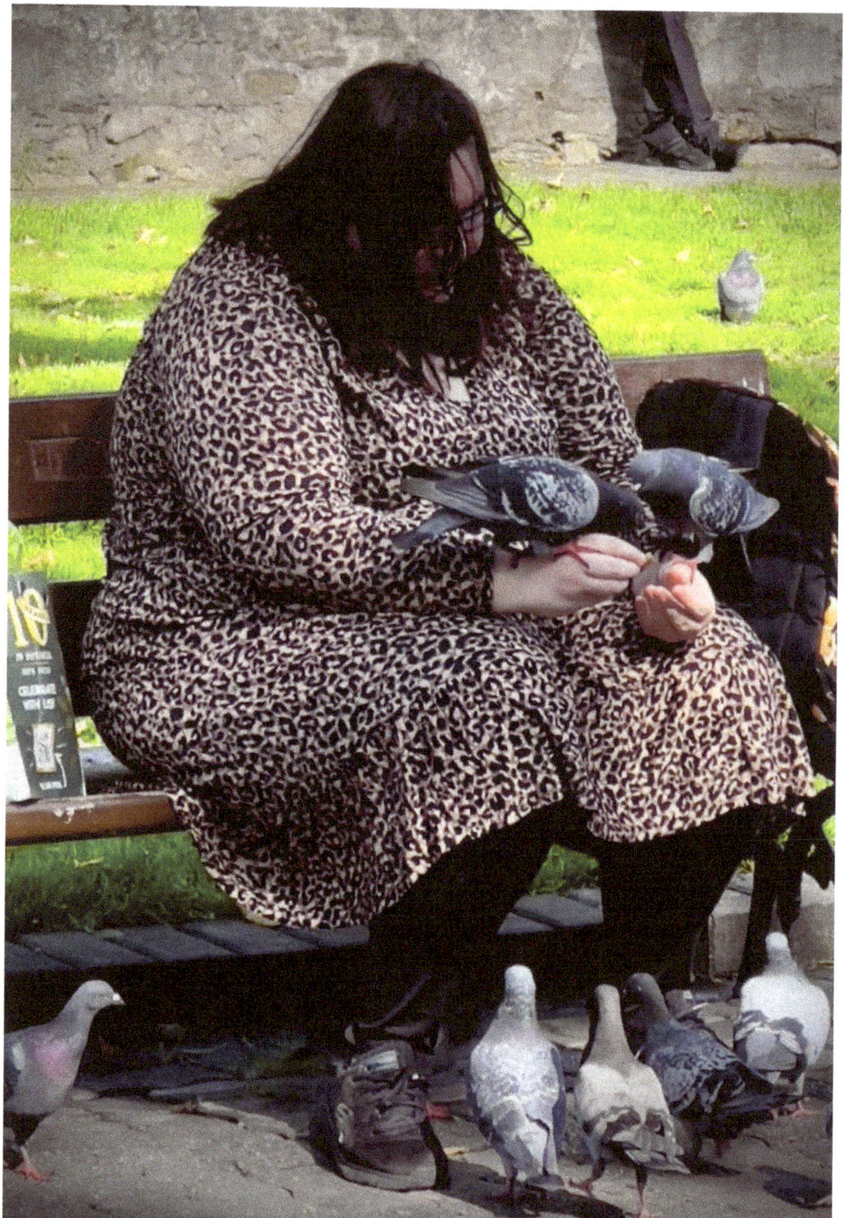

COMPASSION

What is the capacity of the human mind to be compassionate?
Are we able to look at human suffering and grasp what we are seeing?
Do we have the ability to incorporate the hurt of others into the fabric of our being?
Or are we hard wired to look and not see, to observe and not care

I posit the former is the case
However, this is not an innate trait; we are not pre-programmed to see, feel, and respond
It takes practice and a willingness to open our hearts to the pain and suffering of others
It takes openness and an ability to internalize all those things we see as painful

How do we reach this state of heightened awareness?
It is about openness
It is about a willingness to open our hearts and minds
To see, appreciate, and internalize the vulnerability

This is often unpleasant
It is far easier to turn the head and make it go away
But it never does
It is always there and will not disappear
It is part of the fabric of our society

We must learn and teach compassion
We must make it a value, a goal, an attribute desired

Only then will we change the fabric of our society
Only then will we be able to grasp the true social ills
And change them, not because we have to, but because we want to

When we as human beings can truly see and experience the pain
Only then will it begin to lessen

DESPAIR II

The alien creature lives within my body
It travels throughout my blood stream, coursing through me
It touches everything
It will not let me rest

My skin feels like it wants to leave my body
Peeling off me like a painful bandage
Exposing my raw inner self to all
Making me totally vulnerable

I am unable to lose this feeling
It is all-pervasive
And will not let me rest

My mind is feeling the torments of hell
Even the words are hard to draw out

I am at a loss as to what to do.

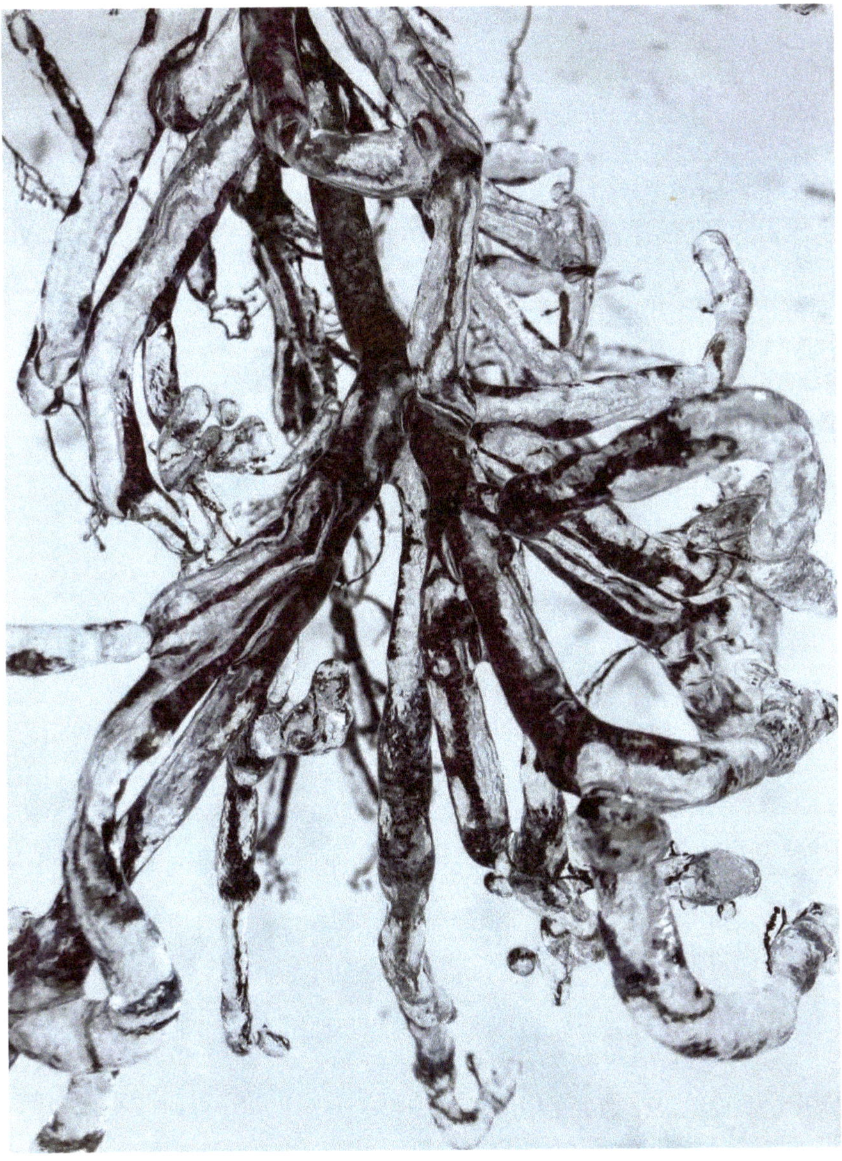

DESPAIR

Every so often, a little bit of light shines through the crack
It illuminates a dark, dreary, room filled with despair
It touches me for only a moment
But it feels so good

Then a cold draft pushes the door closed
And the room loses all warmth and life
It feels damp, dark, musty, and overpowering
It is like the room has the ability to envelope one's mind

It wrings any joy and laughter from my being
It acts like an overwhelming force
That has the ability to suck the essence of life away
It is my enemy, the threat to my existence

I must learn to push the door open
I must learn to walk in the light
I must learn to accept what is
I must find joy in my existence

My body aches for the feeling of passion
That wonderful overwhelming force that catapults one to new heights
That release that occurs throughout mind and body
That wellspring of complete euphoria

How will I capture this again?
Can it ever be with me?
Or am I doomed to ever forsake it?
To languish with this very large hole in my heart?

Is life worth anything without it?
Without it, is there any life at all?
I need to assess

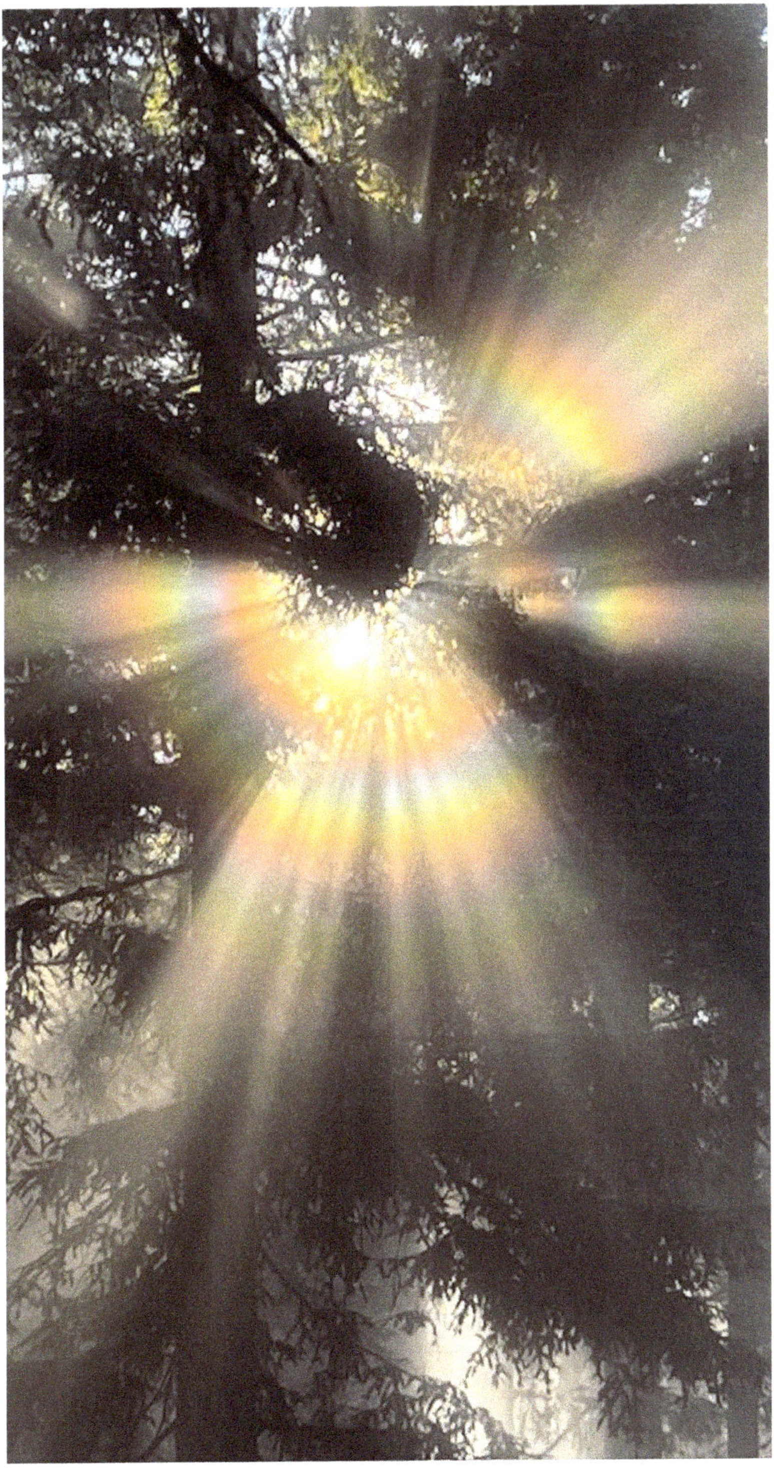

THE ESSENCE OF LIFE

The transience of my life is very much a part of me
It is a tenuous thread which connects disparate pieces of my existence
It is a thread which oftentimes I want to push aside
And other times I want to grab and hold it like a lifeline

It is ever fleeting
Almost gossamer in nature
But when I can grasp it
It is ever so powerful

When I can hold it and bring it to my breast
I can love it and revel in it
I can make it the powerful force
Which frees me and enables me
The force which compels me to act
The force that adds meaning to an often dull existence
The force which makes me the person I can be

Where does that force come from?
It emanates from my love
From the person who enlivens me
Who is able to bring forth the spirit
The life force which when realized
Makes all things beautiful and vital

It is what you add to me
What you stimulate
It is you, my one true love

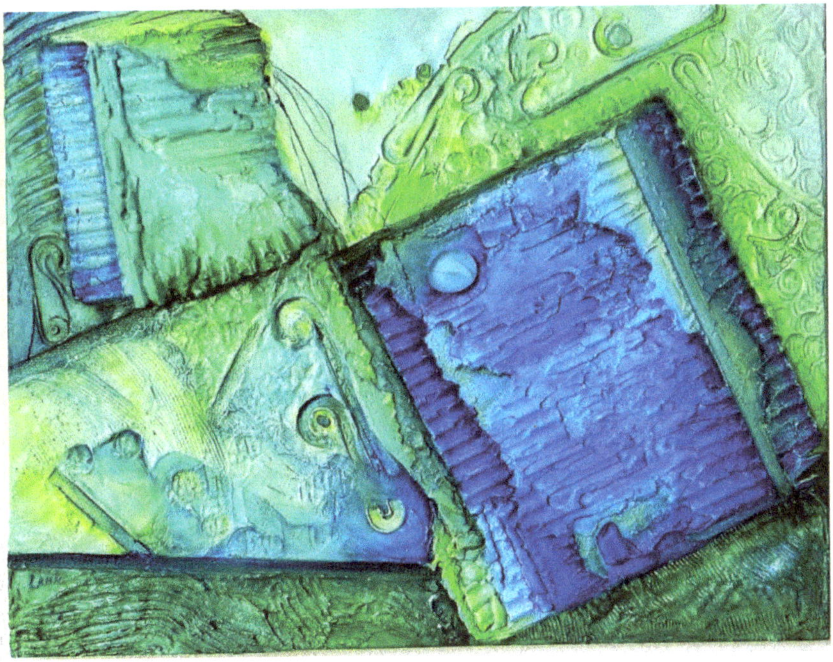

FATE

I wrap the blanket around my shoulders
I take in the warmth and comfort
It soothes me and gives me a feeling of protection
It is my shield, if only against one of the elements of my life

I yearn to pull the blanket around my mind
To soothe the thoughts and the feelings
That race over the gyri like snakes
Causing friction, anxiety, and pain

There doesn't seem to be a mind blanket
Sometimes it exists in a bottle
Sometimes it is a friend's comfort
And sometimes, it cannot be found

It is during these times when it cannot be found
That the depths of the pain and loneliness are present
They actually smother all the efforts to offer solace

The struggle is monumental and at times insurmountable
It will require great effort and endurance
It will define my being
And it will decide my fate

Fate is a strange thing
It is like the future is already written
When actually it plays a small part
We are more the masters of our destiny than the tools of it

The trick is to recognize this, define our fate
And decide to move forward

Do I have the strength of character?
Or do I remain a tool succumbing to the hand of fate?

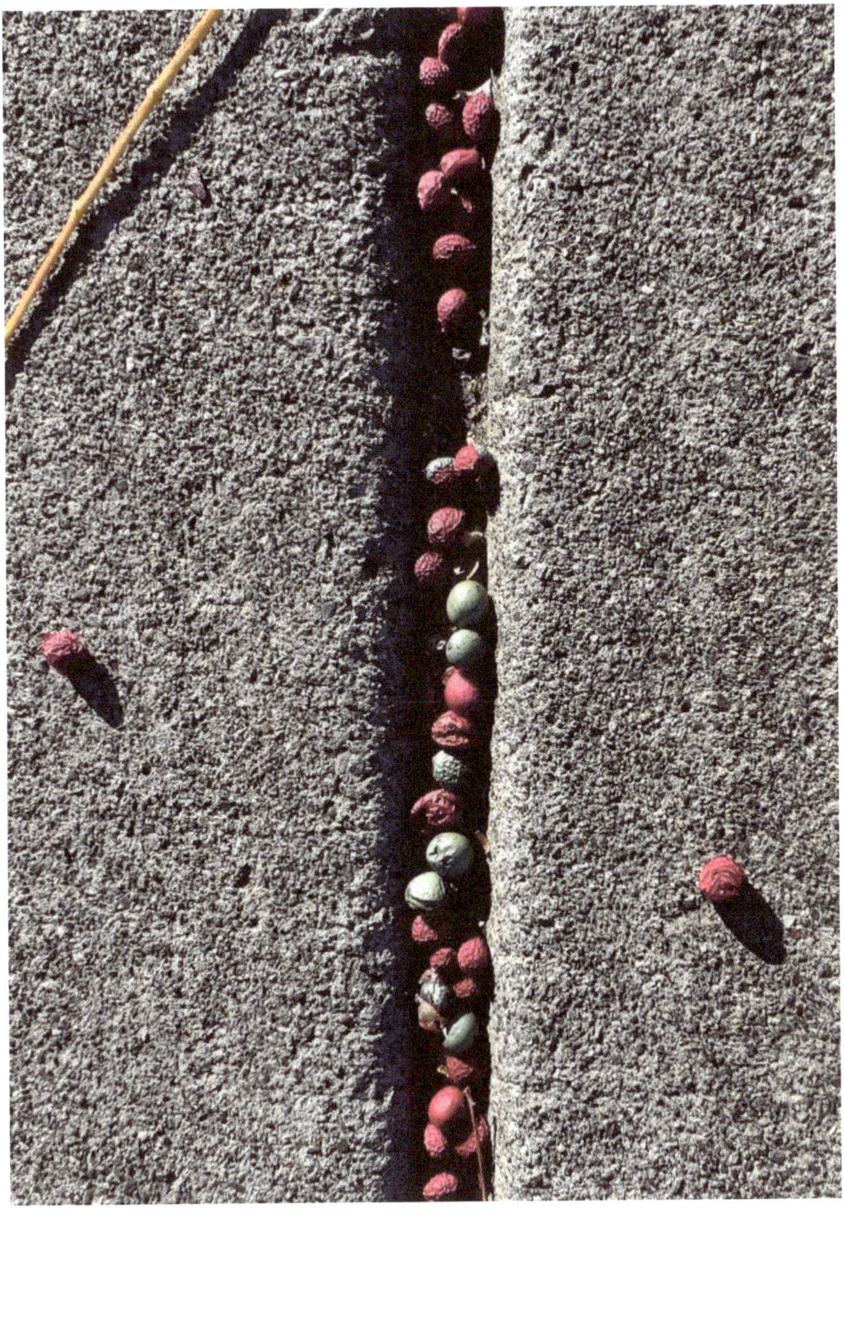

FOUNDATIONS

Relationships are the creation of two minds and hearts coming together
They form a bond that is so very different for each
For some it is tightly woven
Often inextricably entwined like the vine of the forest
For others it is loose and tenuous
Built on a base of sand which seems to be ever shifting

How does one grow and thrive
While the other seems to slip ever so slowly into nothingness?

It is by the force of will

What do you want to create?
What do you have the power to create?
Oftentimes, situations sap our power
They diminish it
They steal it from us

The goal is to see the depth and power of the relationship
To understand its worth to all parties
And to capture that strength and grow it

Nourish it, do not let it starve and wither
Do all in your power to create positivity
Build upon that which is bedrock
And do not let the seepage of despair eat at the foundation

Always look for the joy and the beauty
Use these to shore up any small cracks which the foundation develops

We can create, we can destroy
The choice is ours and not often so apparent

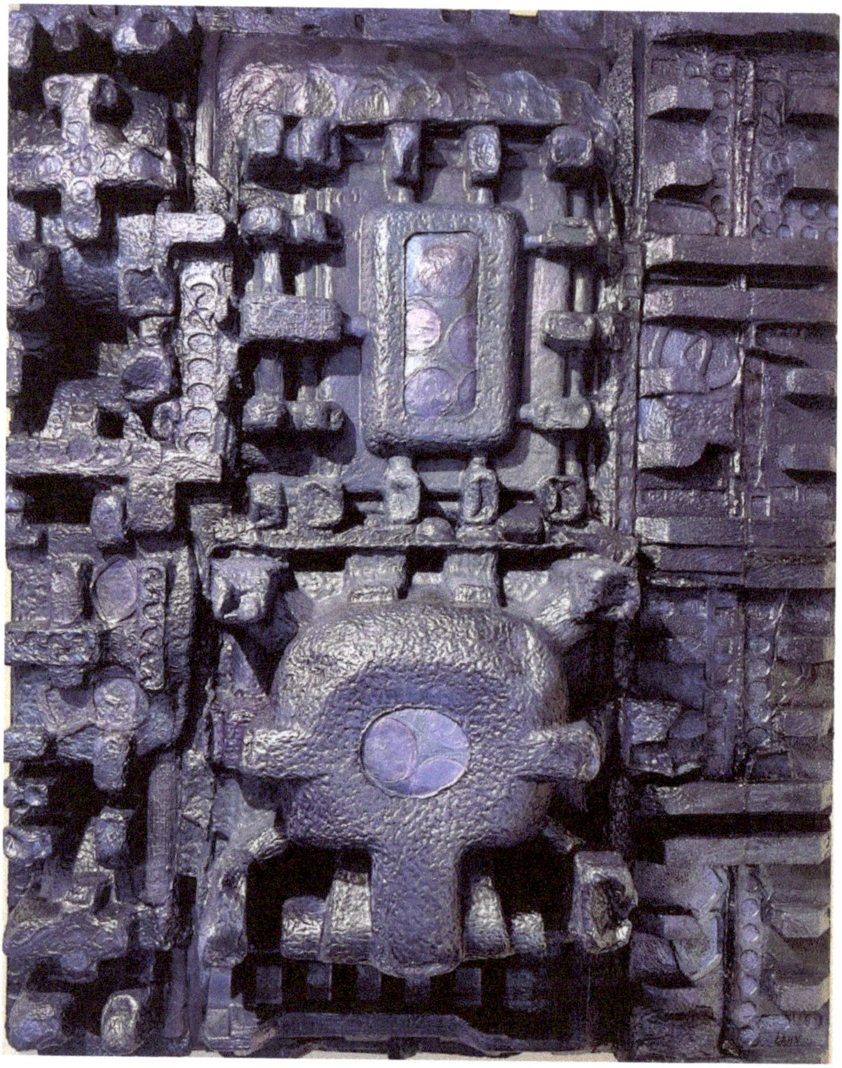

HAPPINESS OR DESPAIR

To reach deeply into the wellspring of tranquility
To understand the emotional triggers and the nuances of balance
This is the ability to regulate that which has the tendency to control
To take control and use it as a powerful tool to enlightenment

Too often the daily onslaught that assails our hearts and minds
Creates a web of feeling and emotion which seems to run amuck
It seems to take control and push our physiologic functions to the breaking point

We must be able to assess the intricacies of the web
We must be able to take apart each strand and deal with it
We have the power and the control
Butall too often we relinquish it to powerful stimuli

If we asses and understand the stimuli, we can influence them
We can sort them, box them, keep them in their proper compartment
Then, as we wish, we can carefully open each and deal with the contents

We must learn to control our emotions and feelings because they are ours
Only then will be able to move forward as we desire
Not at the whim of jumbled emotions

We are human, we have control
We must work to maintain it

The human mind can be an exquisite thing or the ultimate nemesis
It can allow us to create, feel joy, appreciate love and thrive
Or it can take control of our very being and cause us pain

What is the trick we can employ to allow positive to overcome the negative?

It is like a battle between good and evil. Which will survive the conflict?

It is the part we most nourish

HUMAN NATURE

The daisy's are in bloom
Small ferns pop up everywhere
My garden is coming alive

The birds are at my feeder
The squirrels come-destroying my feeder
They leave evidence of their presence is everywhere

I am my gun
A small explosion comes from the muzzle
The squirrel falls, lies dead at my feet
Another body lies among all this beauty-death that I caused

Am I out of tune with the beauty of nature
I wonder and I wait-will the vermin return and cause my response
I question my motivation and my right

Am I human and supreme
Or just an intruder into the world order
Do I have the right to interfere with the grand plan
Or do I need to learn my place.

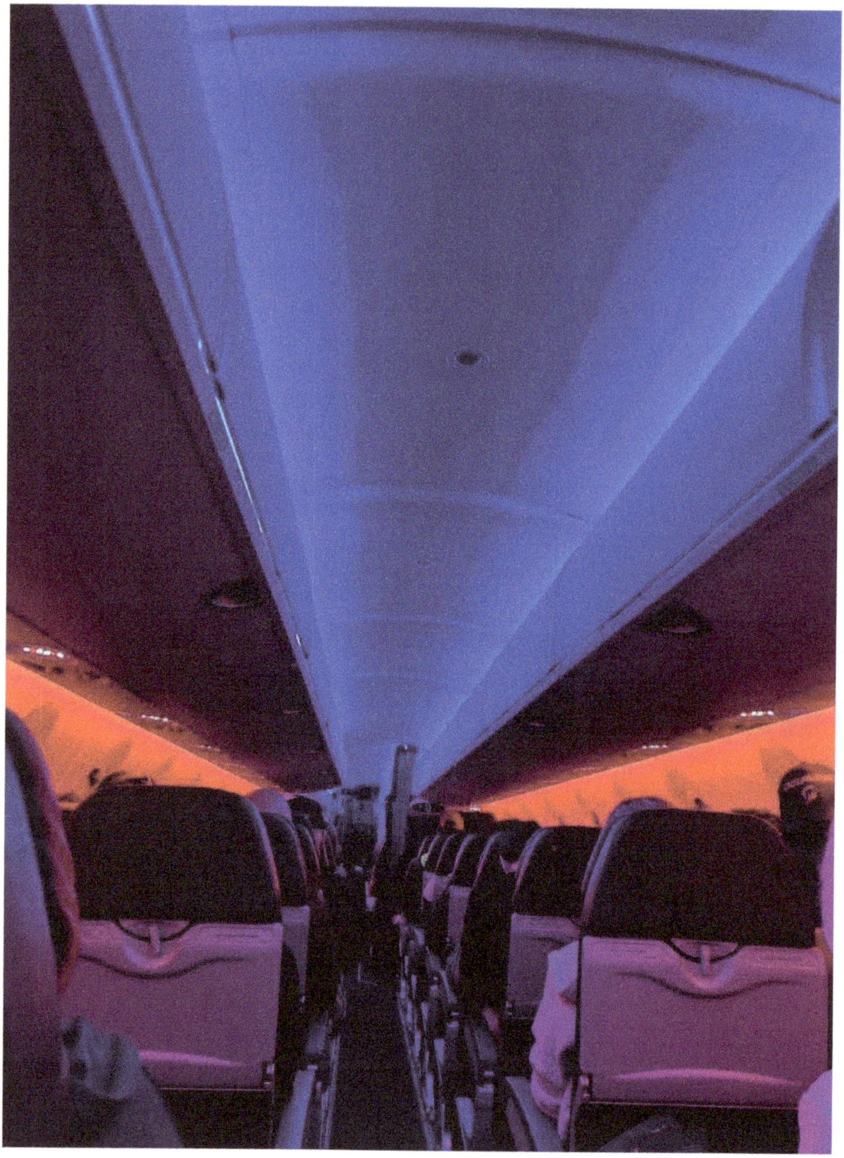

HI HO HI HO

I am on an airplane to Alaska
I am surrounded by over 300 people
Yet, I am so alone

The constant whine of engine and wind
The occasional bump or jolt

And yet, I might as well be in an isolation chamber

No one to talk to
My only interaction is with a woman in uniform
She hates her job
It is easy to tell
I represent only unpleasant tasks

She will fulfill them
But not with joy and caring

It is an inhuman experience

I'd rather walk to work.

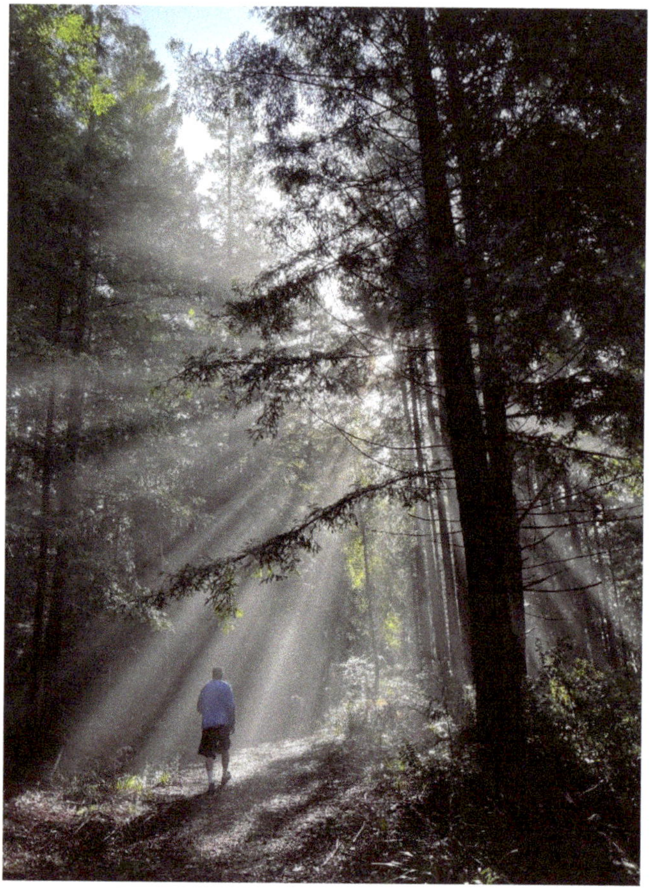

I HAVE WALKED

Can one be in love without another to love?
Can love transcend time and distance?
Can love be preserved in the crucible of loneliness?

I am sure
I have felt the pang of loneliness
And the pressure of the crowd

They may alter the feeling of love
They in themselves cannot break the back of love

For whether alone or in a crowd
I often walk alone

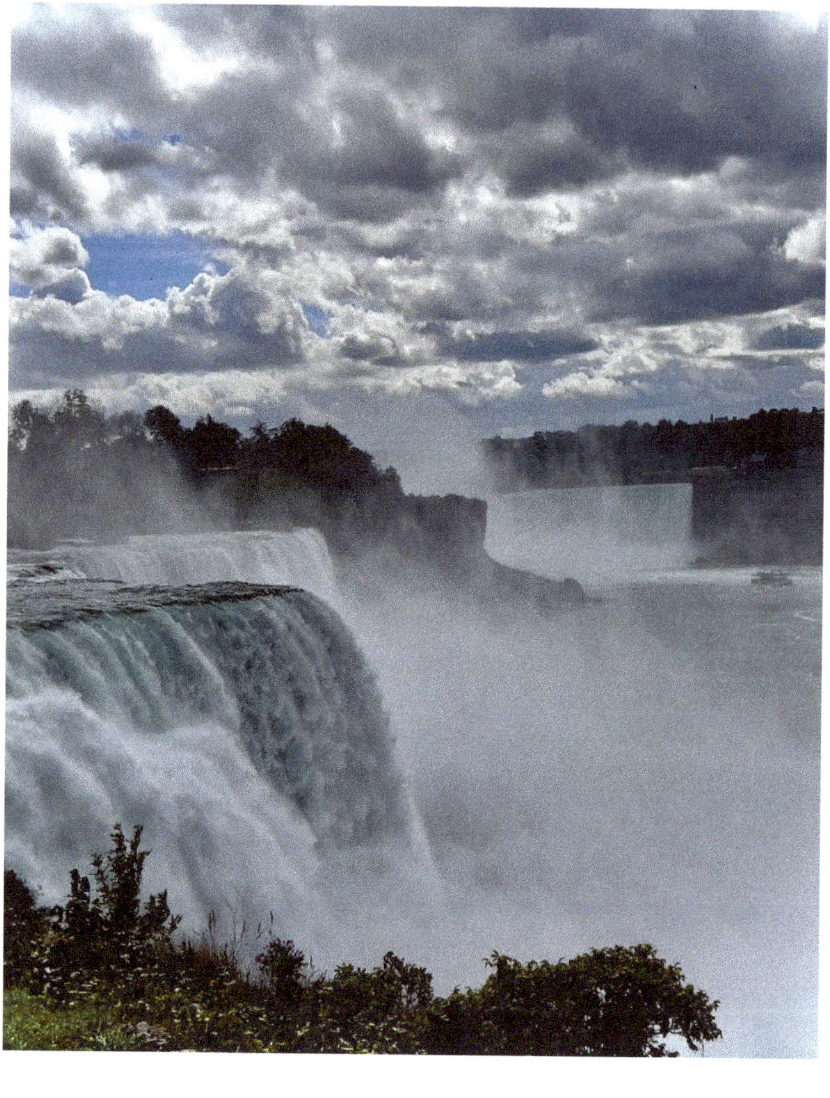

I MISS THE STREAM

The snow-capped beak melts in the spring sun, sending its droplets down to form the runoff
Thus the small stream begins, with its trickle growing in the bright sunlight
The trickle grows, it meets other small outflows and eventually the stream forms
It grows and picks up speed down the mountain
It shimmers in the reflective light and gives voice to the water over the rocks
It is happy, joyful, and it lifts the spirits of those who encounter it

The stream becomes a river
It grows in width and depth and enters the deep forest below
It is no longer bright and playful
But, rather, large and foreboding

Don't get too close
You could easily slip
Being pulled into the raging torrent
Your body, like an egg being bounced about on an unfriendly surface
Cracked and broken, your yolk or precious being slowly oozing into the unforgiving stream

Sometimes when we see only the river and never the stream
All is lost

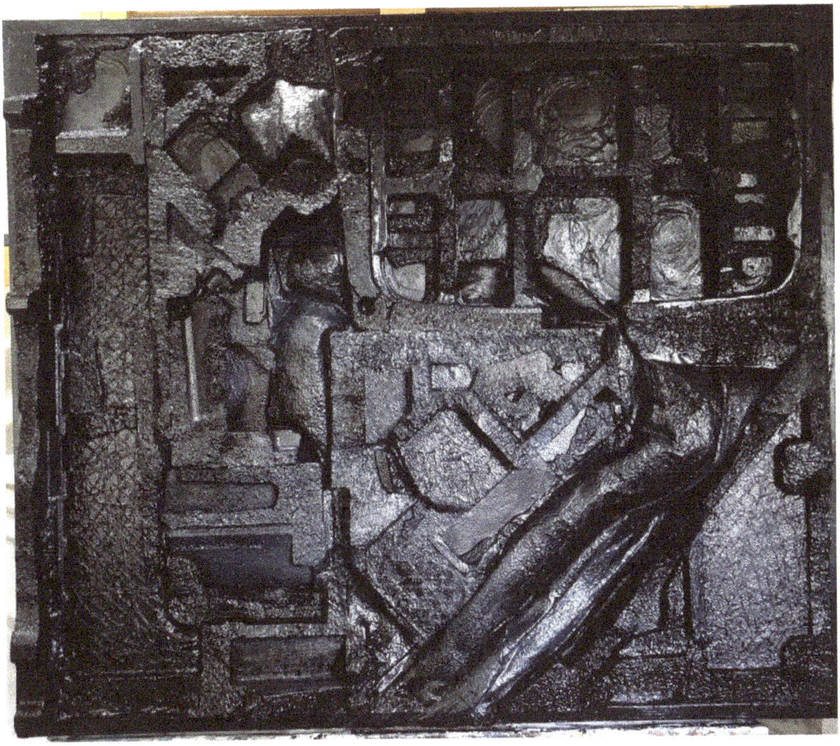

INDECISION AND PAIN

I sit alone feeling the cold wind bite through my clothes
Although covered, I feel unprotected
My anxiety level is high
I am at a loss as to what to do

It is a feeling of desolation and loneliness
An empty feeling which gnaws at my innards
I cannot find a place of shelter
All directions lead to emptiness

There is a beacon of light in the distance
It shines bright and draws me in
I could walk toward it or stay
I know not what to do
I am afraid

Who will help me make my choice?
Who can help me make my choice?
Only I have the power to change it
And I struggle so with the dilemma

When will I get my chance to walk in the sun?
Only when I can unlock the door to happiness
That door that dwells deep within me

Oh, where is the key?

LEARNING

The small sparrow pecked at the purple crocus
Its head popping out of the snow-covered ground
The sun causing it to catch my eye as I pass
I watch with wonder, the rebirth of the world

How many times in the last months
Have I walked by and not noticed?
How many times have I missed a moment of joy?
How many times have I not seen my lover?

Life is meant to be lived and experienced
It is not a painful trip to death
I must learn to reawaken my sensitivities
I must learn to live

I know how
Now I must do

LIFE

I sit and watch the spider move back and forth and spin his web
He moves in a pattern, swift and sure to build the construct
Stopping and starting in small, bursts of construction
Ever cognizant of the final product.

He is driven by some unknown gene to plan, construct and utilize his web
To rest, capture, kill, and eat

There really is no difference between the spider and mankind
We are fascinated by something we also do on a daily basis
We just don't see or internalize it
We have separated ourselves from reality
Society is now our blanket of protection.

The individual is no different from the Spider

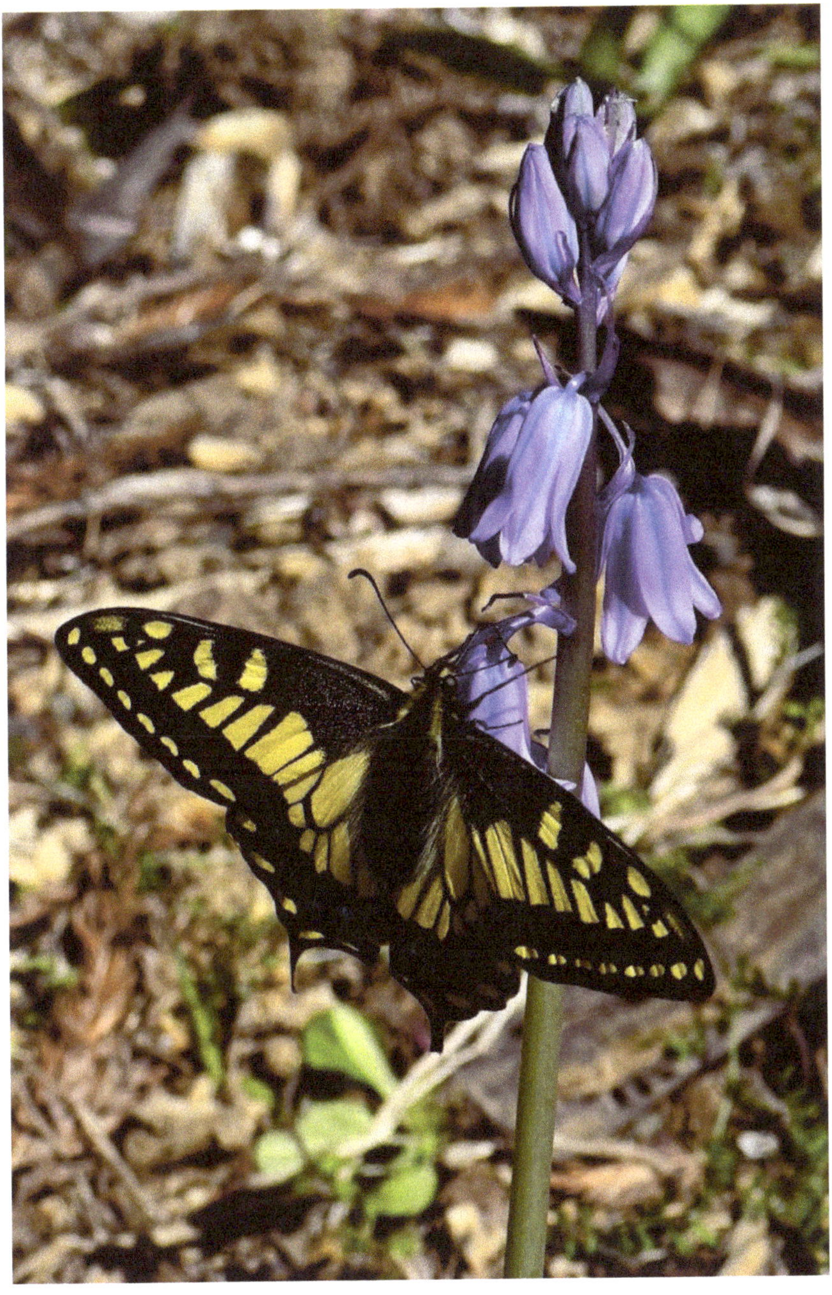

LIFE'S MOMENTS

Why do we allow ourselves to fall into the deep, wet, dark, slimy pit?
Why are we unable to climb the muddy wall, always falling back?
Why do we lie at the bottom, the rain soaking us through, unable to move?
Why can't we rise up and conquer the pit, master the seemingly endless torture?

We are paralyzed by our indecision
We are unwilling to face the difficult choices that face us and to deal with them
We are the product of our human failings
We are of loose moral fiber, unable to move because of our fear

Our fear of causing hurt
Our fear of being honest with ourselves and others
Our fear of exposure, of being seen as we really are
Our fear that the carefully constructed house of cards will fall

How can we overcome this seemingly endless battle?
Only by opening the door to truth and letting in the light
Allowing the parts to be seen and to be explained
Allowing the pieces to fall into the places where they finally fit

Humans often have difficulty fitting their feelings into reality
Reality often robs us of the ability to be totally free, it constrains us
It is, however, what surrounds us
It is the hard, cruel fact of what is

What we must do to escape the pit
Is to clearly understand what we face
And be steadfast in that determination not to succumb
Learn to find the love and joy which is under the mud
Be strong enough to grab it, savor it, and relish the fact that we

have it

Appreciate what two people have the ability to give one another
Not what the world can do to rob them of that gift

Remove the dark, oppressing, hurtful feelings
Fill your heart with love, caring, compassion, and forgiveness
Be open to the joy and celebrate every moment
Because the number of moments are finite

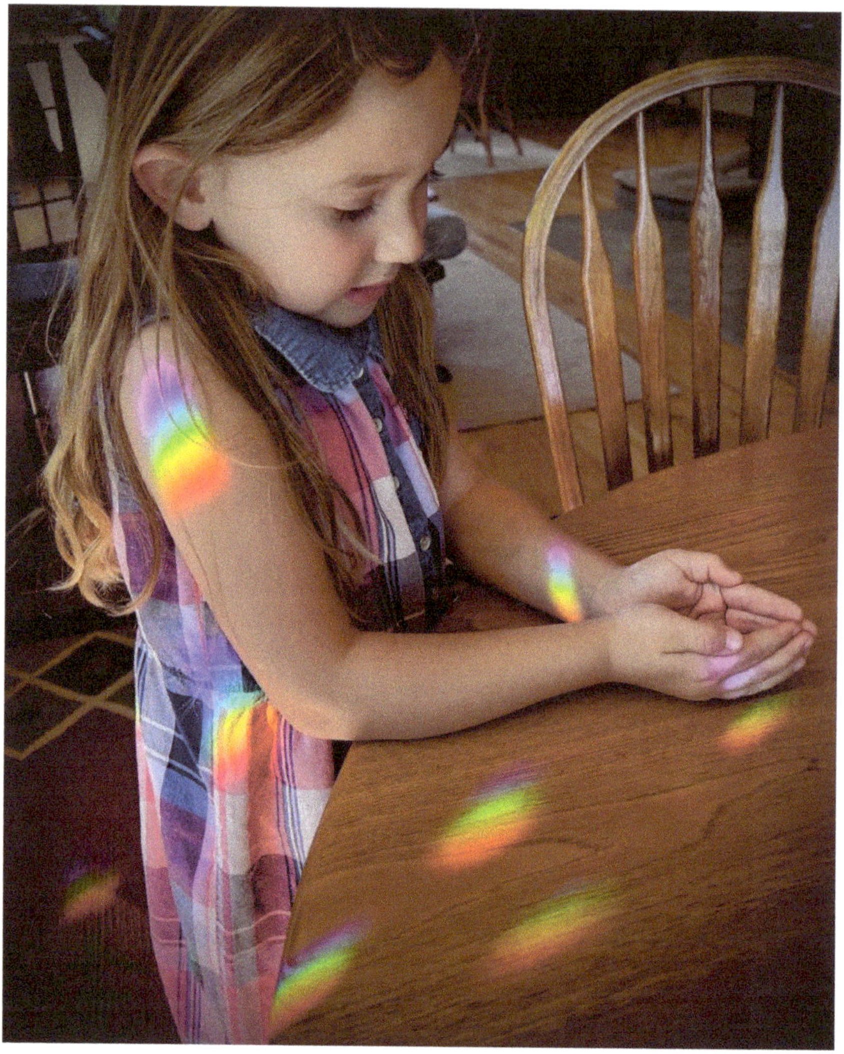

LIVE AS A CHILD

Why do we struggle so with our everyday existence?
Why is life so often a challenge and not an adventure?
Why do we add constraints to those things which happen so naturally?
Why do we not allow our hearts and minds to absorb and enjoy the treasures that surround?

Why, because we are human
We have created a mindset which imprisons us
A mindset which constricts rather than expands
A mindset that does not allow the best in us to come forth

We must learn to be free
Free of the bonds which tend to shackle us
Free from the preconceived notions that imprison us
Free to let our beings grow and nourish themselves from the joys and pleasures of life

We need to attain the joy and wonder of children
That innate ability to be curious, inquisitive, and always seeking
Not closed down, not constricted
Rather like a delicate flower that sees the sun and opens to it
Like a bee that goes from the sweetness of flower to flower

We must shed some of our human shackles
We must shed that which stifles us

Assume the mantle of love
Look at everything as something to be treasured
Look at your gifts not your crosses to bear

Be human but be a child again

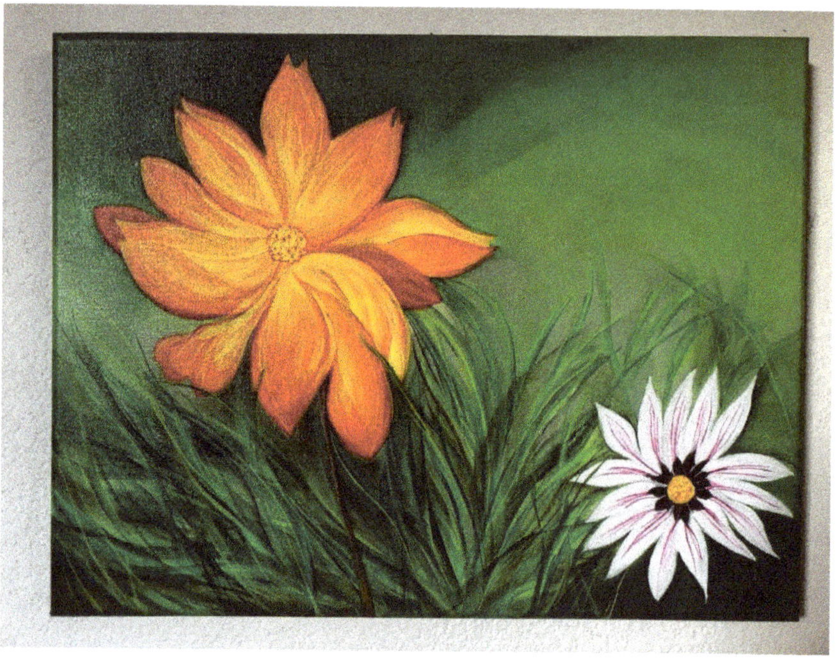

LONELINESS

When the seeds of loneliness are planted
And days with no direction grow and grow
The seeds flourish. They grow like weeds
Clouding the senses and creating an overwhelming sense of sadness

And when clarity comes forward and expose the seeds
They slowly begins to shrink
Now possibilities open where before there was only darkness
The sunlight clears the mind and allows it to be free

A person who goes through life alone
Is a person incomplete. A person stifled. A person not alive.
And when that unfulfilled part is completed
A person blossoms and grows
Open to heights never imagined

You have opened that door
You have let the light shine in
You have completed me with your love

The flower springs forth
And the world is bathed in its beauty

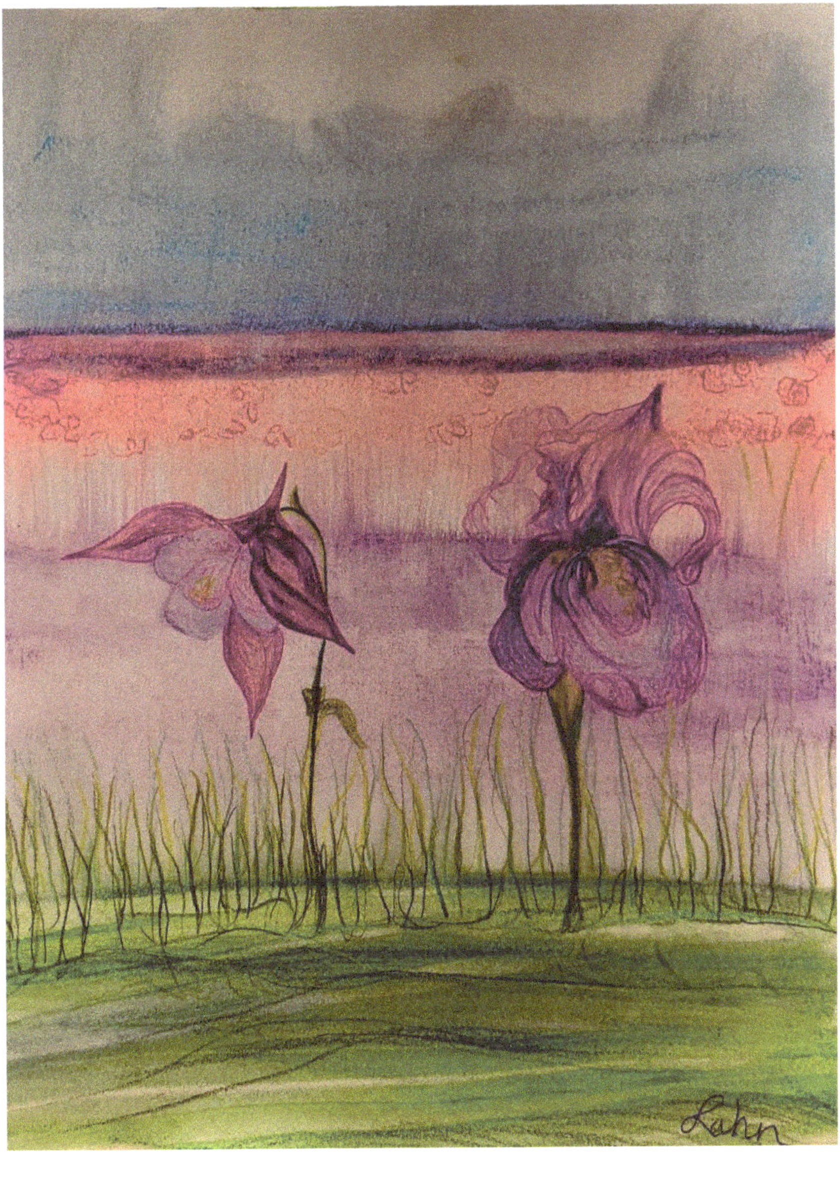
Lahn

MY AWAKENING

I feel free and in love
My very fiber aches for you
I long for your words, your touch, your smile
Your gentle caress of my hand in yours

I can see you, so soft, loving, and giving
I see you in the morning light and the gentle shades of twilight
I see you walk through the door
Your smile, your warmth, your settling presence

I want you with me always
In joy, in sorrow, in happiness and in pain
I long to touch you, I long to possess you

To take you in my arms
To gently stoke your warm flesh
To feel you melt into my being
To open the door that has been closed too long

To open my heart, my being, my soul
To ignite in me the passion only you can instill

You are my world, my reason for life
My muse, my lover, my dearest friend
You are everything
You are the reason for my being
You are my one true love
I want you, I need you
You complete me

MY MORNING

I gaze over the expanse of water of the pond
The light has arrived but not the sun
A heavy mist covers the water
The world is waking up and the symphony of birds comes alive
The dense mist almost looks surreal

Squirrels and chipmunks are running to and fro
Ever searching for the morning meal

The fog thickens – only the sound of distant cars can be heard
Slowly the road in the distance is gone – covered by the thick fog

All becomes quiet yet much of the world awakens
Awaiting the morning light – the Sun
All will change and another picture will appear
I am at peace – alone except for the circling hawk and symphony of birds

OJO CALIENTE I

The soft flow of the water
Gurgling in the warm, sensuous pool

In the background
The adobe cliffs
Jagged and unyielding

The sparse vegetation holding on for life
Awaiting the life giving rain

The tranquility
Almost roaring in my ears

Lulling me into a soft all-encompassing trance

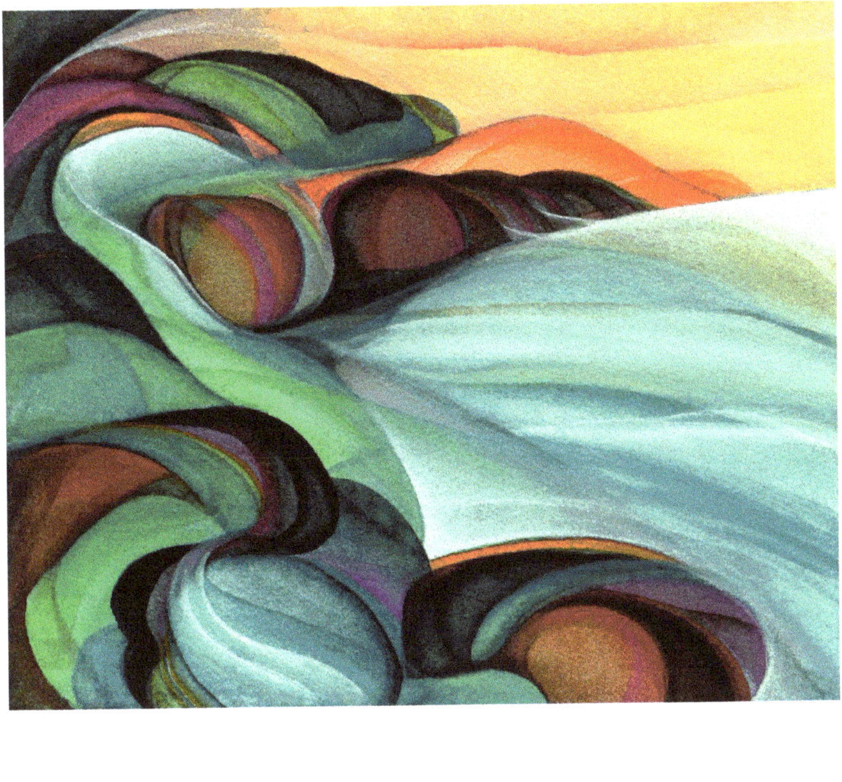

OJO CALIENTE II

The large red-winged dragonfly
Circles the sparse vegetation like
A miniature biplane

A small fly circles my hand
Lands, looks, takes a step, and heads for my foot

I am alone in nature
With only the sound of water, wind, and thought

While the marshmallow clouds
Block the blazing sun

I take off my hat to wipe my brow
And the water drips slowly down my cheek

I cover my face with the red bandana
Pour some water from my canteen
Look into the vast landscape
And ride on

Although I see no other living creature
I am not alone

My presence diminishes in the presence
Of so much that I do not control

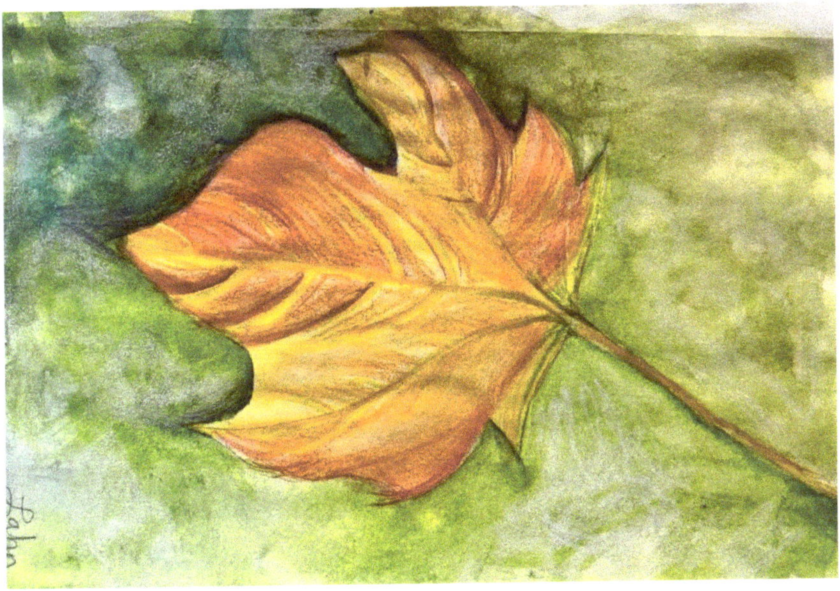

OLD CAPE COD

I walk the empty dunes in November
The last traces of summer linger as only a memory
I hold your hand and draw you close to me
You warm me like the summer sun
And I feel joy in my heart

The beaches are empty and the restaurants are closed
Yet the sounds and the smell of the Cape are everywhere
In our aloneness they envelop us
Surrounding us in a layer of comfort and joy
Which brings us alive and makes our solitude all the more joyful

We are in love
In love with life
We only see the beauty that surrounds us
Not the emptiness of a season passed
Only the fullness of a life to begin

We are in love

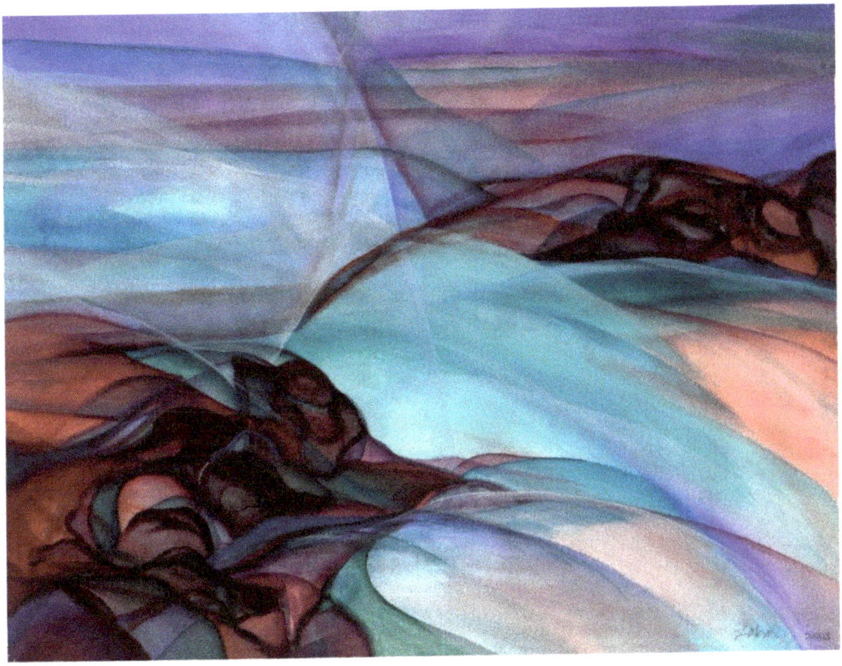

OPENING THE DOOR

Today I awoke and the pit in my stomach was gone
I am restless and awoke early but not with such great apprehension

I feel that my grief has been soothed and does not burn with the usual intensity

It started last night

As she walked in the door, tears came to my eyes and my heart lifted
I gazed at her face and took her in my arms

Although I cried, the world was suddenly safe
I was in a place of refuge with my best friend and lover

We caressed, kissed ever so tenderly, and looked at each others' eyes
We did so for a long time

We were both apprehensive
We are both very much in love
We are both where we should be

The experience of last night will have impact on us, some positive and some with pain
Only we will be able to sort it out

I got much comfort
I hope I have caused no grief

OUT OF AFRICA

The open plains stretch endlessly before the eye
The tall grass waves in the breeze like seaweed at the ocean shore
The animals wander, almost aimlessly, across the great Savannah
The world is alive
And death is everywhere

The need for food and the quest for life are everywhere
One eats the other to preserve the chain of life
The apparent peaceful calm is frequently broken by the cries of pain
The pain of one life giving itself so another may live
And death is everywhere

As the rains come and go there is a constant rebirth of life
The brown becomes green and the dry becomes lush
New birth is everywhere
The young romp and play while awaiting mothers' food
Mothers hunt and bring life-giving sustenance to their young
And death is everywhere

The beauty of equatorial Africa is limitless
It surrounds you with its sights, smells, sounds, and tastes
It opens the senses and floods the mind
It creates a picture of unrivaled beauty
And death is everywhere

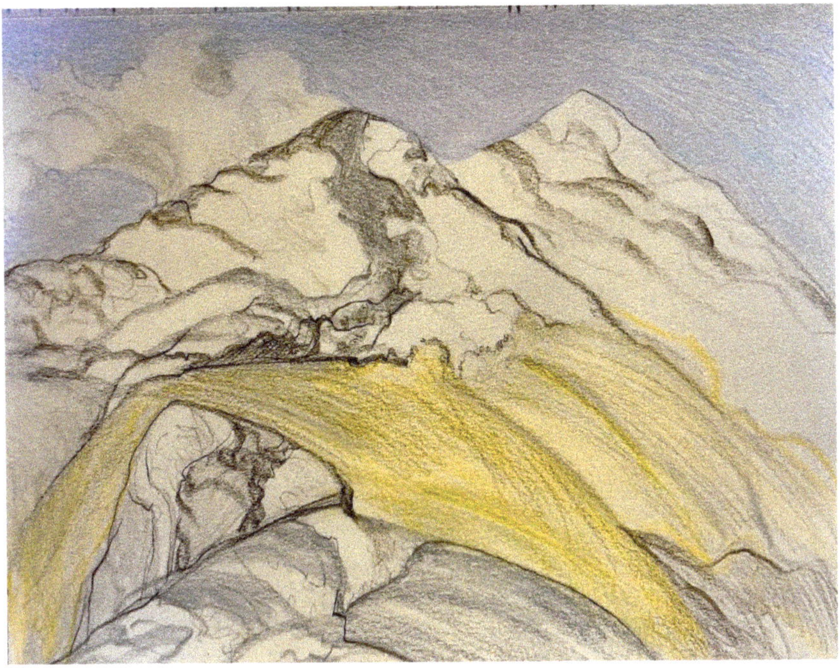

SANDIA MOUNTAINS

The blue dark patches splash over the deep green
Dancing clouds cast shadows that alter the pallet in ever-changing hues
And always the blue of the sky butts against it in sharp contrast

It is as if someone pushed the jagged peaks up from the dark foreground below
Almost as if they ripped into the brown dessert and were seeking a better place

And, always, the red fire of the sun
Works with clouds and sky
To create an ever changing panorama

It is an evolving picture which never remains static
A picture which raises the eye
Into a constant peeking

A symphony of color that goes from Baroque to Classical at an ever-changing pace
It is nature's symphony, ever-changing, ever-playing
And always evolving

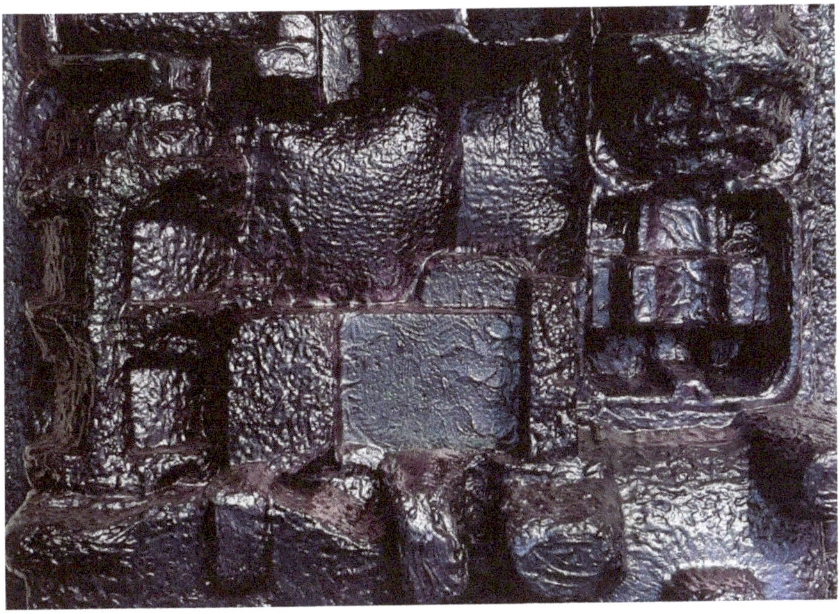

SO WHAT

The daylight is faltering, as I reach for my key
I open the door to my apartment, and it is dark and cold
I flip on the light and the warmth fills the room
Exposing the emptiness I find there
I am home. So what?

Where will I find a place of refuge?
A quiet sanctuary of peace, love, and joy
A haven in the storm of life
A place that makes no longer afraid

I seem to have lost this place
It used to exist
It used to protect me
Now I am alone
In the cold, in the dark, in the loneliness

The question to be asked
Is it worth coming home?

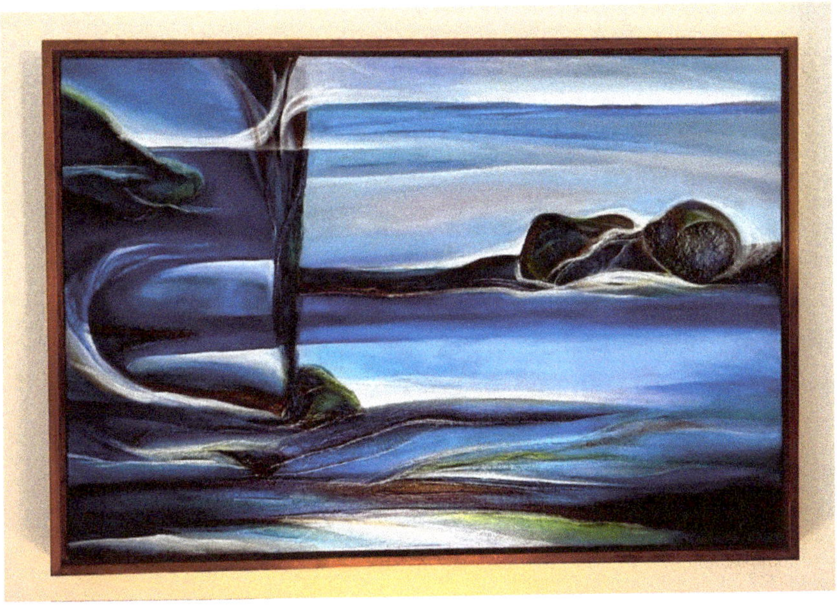

THE CHAMBERS OF MY MIND

The clear sky sparkles above the greens and blues of the turbulent surf
The lazy gull flits about, diving and swooping in the quest for a never-ending food source
The surf beats upon the grey-brown rocks of the craggy shore
And I sit, with my back to the wind, mesmerized by the quietude of my surroundings

My thoughts flit back and forth and like dancing bubbles of the surf
I am lost in a world of sound, sight, smell, and natural beauty
My mind is free from the stresses of my usual chaotic existence
The assault of beauty is a cleanser for the dark, and often painful, emotions of daily life

How easy it is to become obsessed by the dark, brooding, oppressive thoughts of life
How easy it is to be a captive in the dark recesses of the mind
And how hard it is to find the key that can unlock the dark prisons
And release us to the joy and beauty of the natural world around us

It is this beauty which has the power to elevate us to a higher plane
To a place where expansiveness replaces the binding constraints of the very mundane

We must learn the lesson of childhood
The lesson to experience, to touch, feel, smell and be inquisitive about what surrounds us

The gull circles and floats softly, silently, by my ear
I feel the rush of the air as he passes my head
I hear the crash of the surf against the rocks
And taste the salt of the air as I breathe it in

I am in the enlightened chambers of my mind
The door to darkness is temporarily closed
Oh, if only I could keep it that way

THE DARKNESS

The darkness rolls into my room like a humid mist
It envelopes everything, turning it into a grey, brown ooze
It actually sucks the air and the life from the room
It smothers but does not kill. It creates suffering, not death

It permeates my mind, my body, my soul
Extracting all that is beautiful and joyful
Leaving an expanse of desolate wasteland
Strewn with the corpses of pain and suffering

THE END

I hear the hoof beats thundering on the hard-packed dirt
Digging deep with each step
Tearing the sparse vegetation into shreds like a thousand scythes

My blood pumps HARD through my veins
They bulge and strain from the load
A load much greater than can be foreseen
They too are about to be torn asunder

The pain and cloud surrounds the brain
Pushing against its tight covering
Never letting it expand or be still

Constantly pushing
Straining all the resources
Making everything work well beyond capacity

On and on the thundering hoofs march
Ever-beating the soft underbelly of the earth.
And then it ends

Just as suddenly as the horses came, they disappear
And so does the soft tissue of the brain
The skull explodes
And all is scattered and destroyed

The hard edge of the bullet has done its job
All is right with the universe

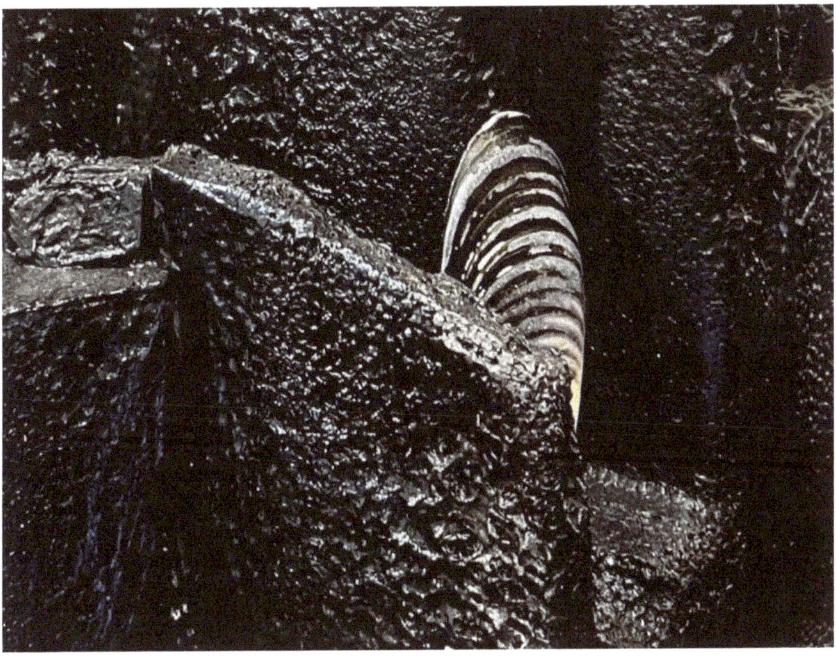

THE ENDLESS JOURNEY

It is an endless walk down a dark, damp corridor
The walls are close as if to confine the space and the being
The floor is uphill, slowly climbing always a little more, making each step ever so challenging
It feels endless

There is no light. Just what the eye adjusts to and yet never enough
Ahead a turn…into a blind corridor
A maze of mind and body
How the body tires, always ready to stop
But nowhere to rest
Only darkness, frustration, and hopelessness

How long is it possible to take this walk?
How long before it is time to sleep?
To lie down, to give up the quest

It could be restful to fall into sleep
Allow the mind to open and expand
To picture the sunlight, the sky, the birds, the trees
To finally free the mind. To be at peace
Oh, it has been so long.

I so miss it

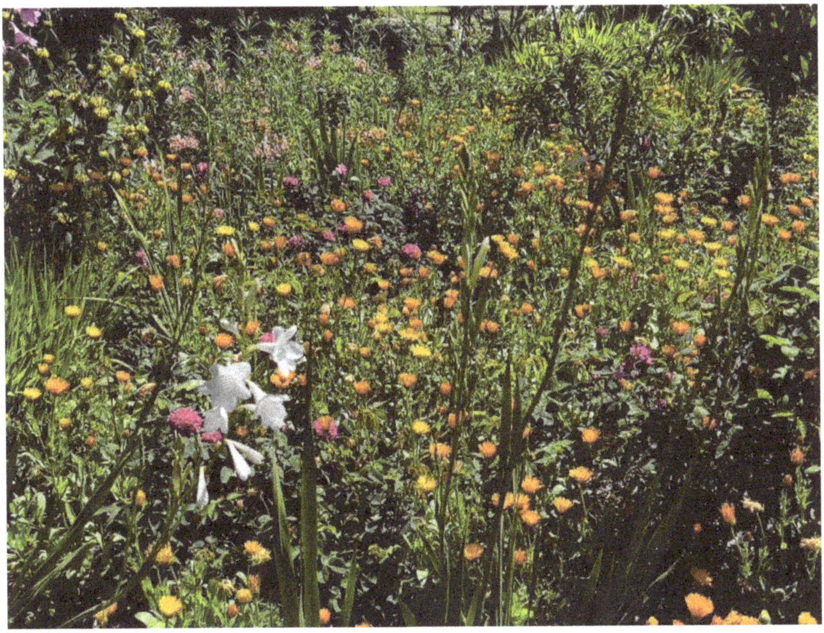

THE GARDEN

When the seeds of loneliness get planted
And days with no direction, grow and grow
The seed flourishes. It grows. It is like a weed

And when clarity comes forward and exposes the seed
It slowly begins to shrink
New possibilities open where before was only darkness
The sunlight clears the mind and allows it to be free

A person who goes through life alone
Is a person incomplete. A person stifled. A person not alive
And when the unfulfilled part is completed
A person blossoms and grows
Often to heights never imagined

You have opened that door
You have let the light shine in
You have completed me with your love

The flower springs forth
And the world is again beautiful

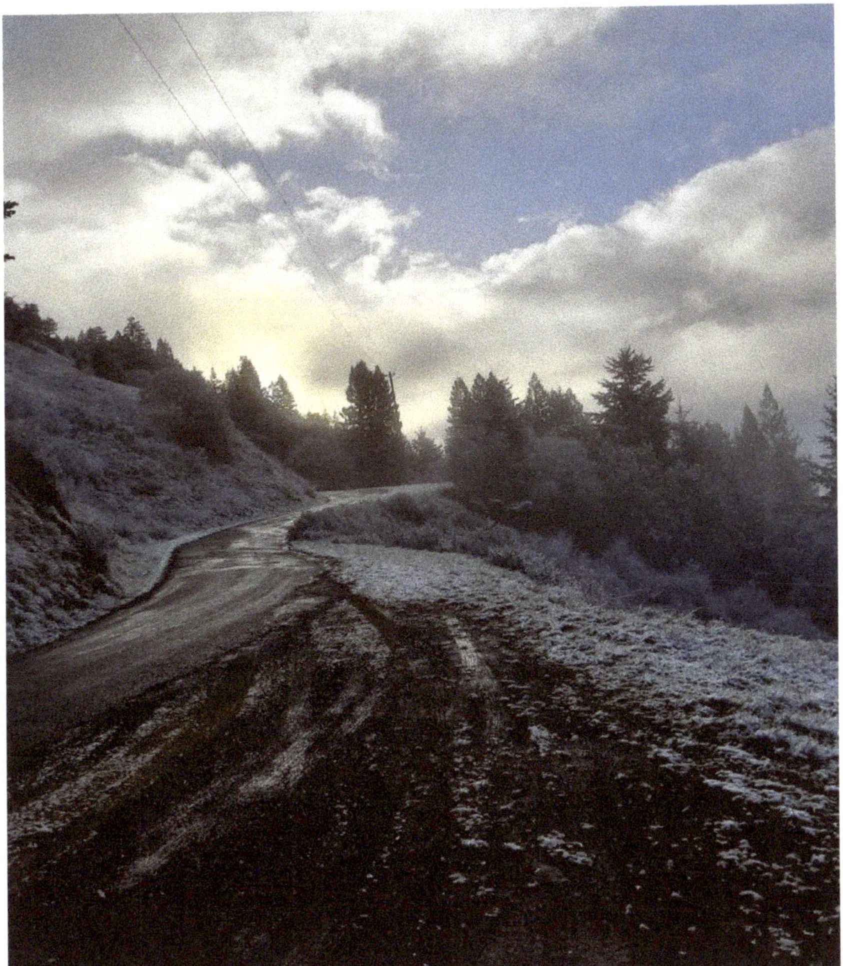

THE HARDEST CLIMB

He walks through the rocky, tree strewn countryside
Stumbling over rocks and crags, jumping over the fallen limbs
His gait is unsteady
The landscape is unforgiving

His boots slip and he grabs a branch
He falters but does not fall
The terrain gradually rises, forever going up
The way is steep, uncertain, and dangerous

Where the path leads no one knows, it does is not marked
Yet he continues to climb, fighting the need to quit
Each step is uncertain, and each step becomes more difficult
He must go on; he knows not why; yet he persists

The summit appears in the mist
As the clouds break, he sees small bits and pieces of it
The distance looks doable, yet he is so tired

The question is what he will do when he reaches the peak?
What will be there? What will he see when the clouds break and the sun shines through?
Will it be worth the trip?

There is another route
Will it be easier?

No one knows

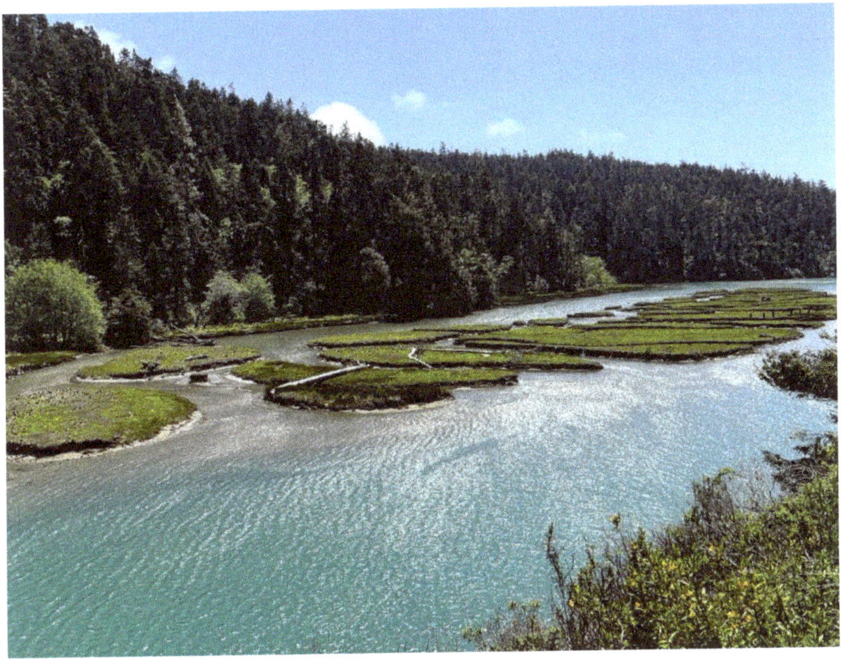

THE JOY OF LONELINESS

I am lost in a world of nature and oneness
Civilization has not crept this way

There are few outside forces
Binding me and my thoughts

I am at peace
I have left the world behind
If only for a short time

Not sure I want to return
To lose this feeling of calm
To subject my soul to the chore of living.

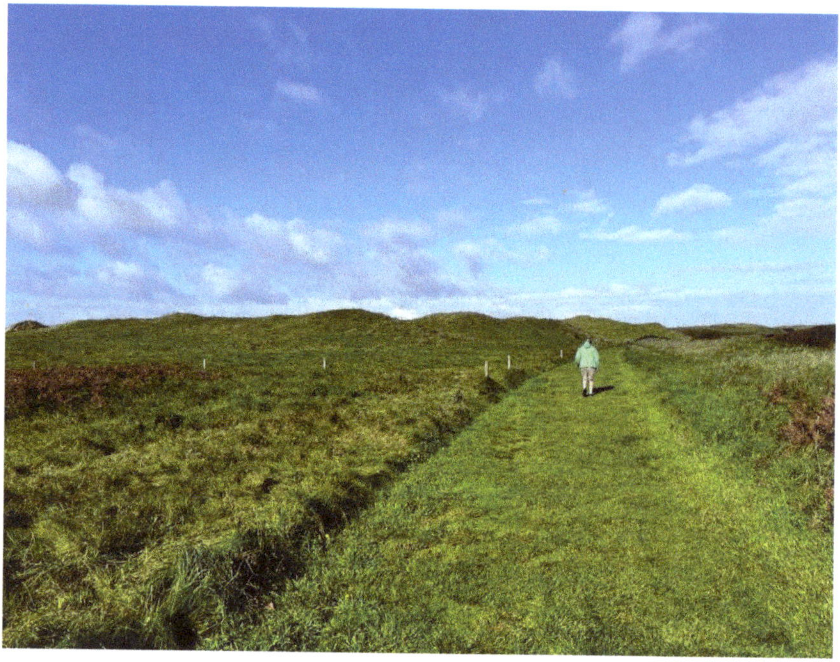

THE LONG WALK

A man often walks a hard path
He tries his best, he does what is expected
He has mate, children, friends, and a job

All give him joy
And all give him angst

He does his best
He trudges along
Is it appreciated . . . or expected

What lies at the end of the path?
Peace, contentment, and rest
 Or exhaustion, sorrow, and grief

He does not know
So he continues his journey
Or does he….

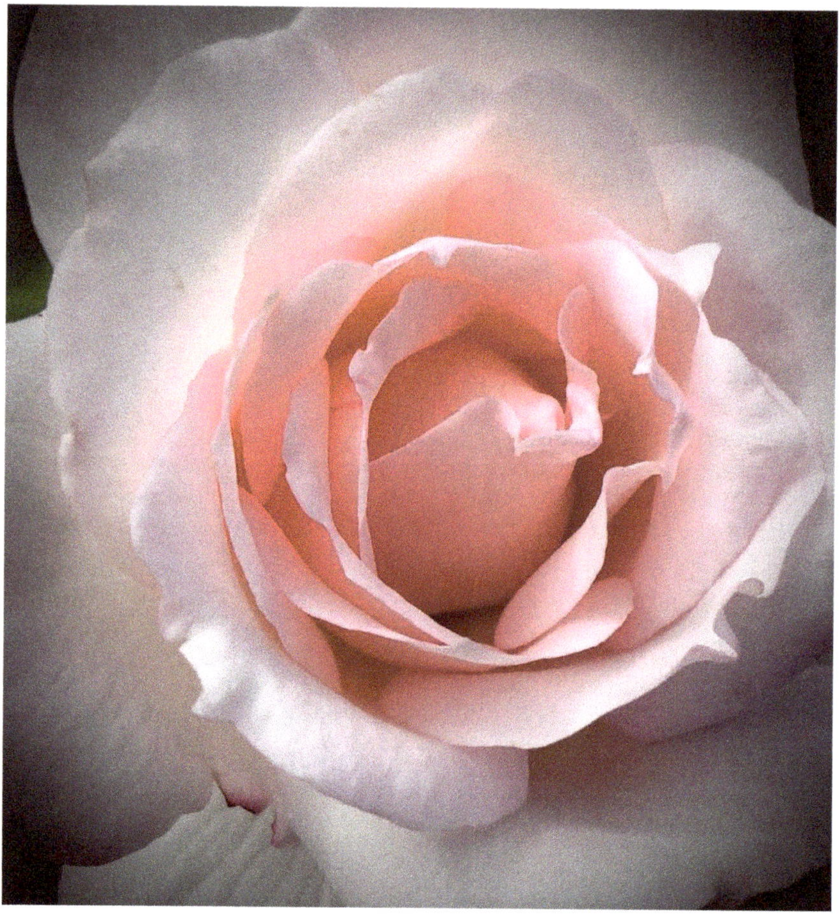

THE RELEASE OF LOVE

I picture your face and I smile
The warmth you project
Grabs me and pulls me toward you

I long to hold you, kiss you, possess you
To feel your warm flesh against mine
To feel the depth of your breath as I caress your skin

I am a prisoner to your power, your love
It envelops me like a warm blanket on a cold winter night
It covers me and gives me comfort
Igniting my soul in a sea of fireworks
Causing my skin to glow and tingle

The soft light covers our entwined bodies
Creating the shadow of one being
Two souls coming together, blending into one

You have such power over me
You control my every emotion
Like a roller coaster of love
Slowly up and then cascading down, losing all sense of position

I love the feeling of losing myself
In the web of your embrace
The total feeling of submission
And the total feeling of being loved and desired
It is all encompassing

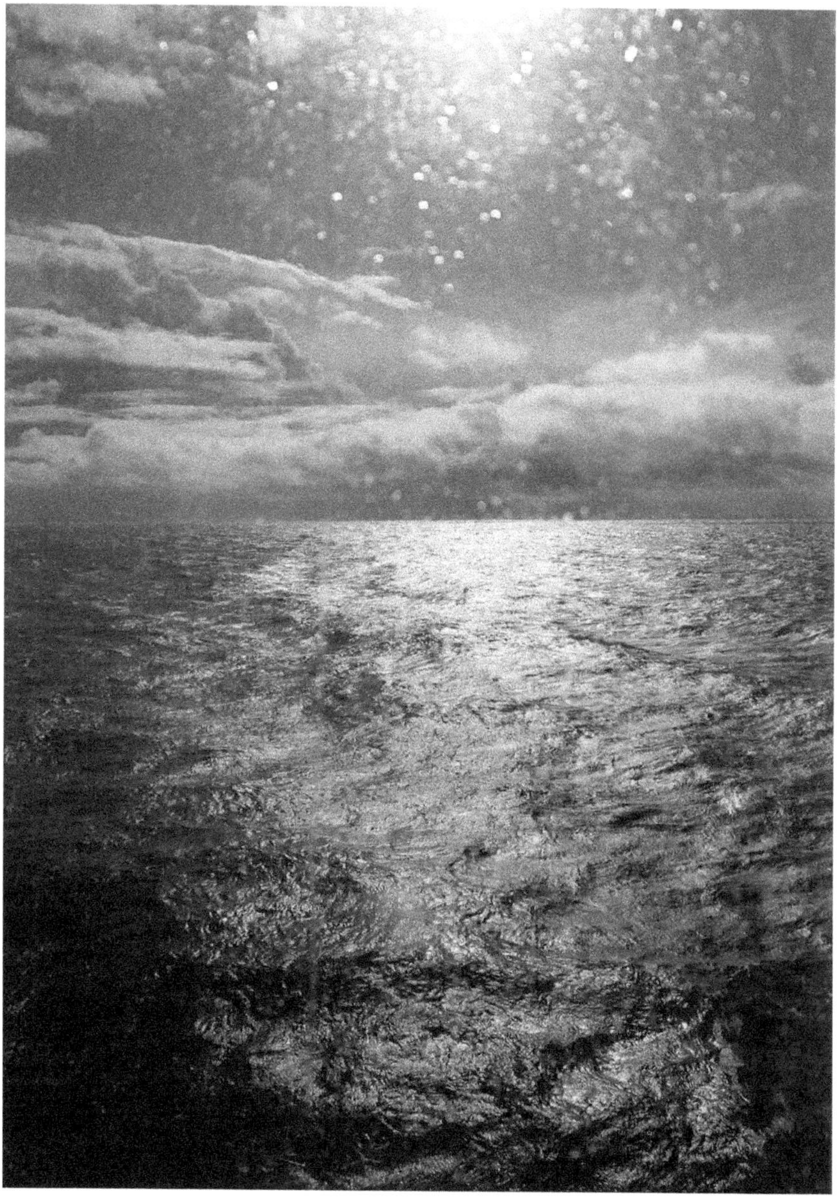

THE SAILOR'S LAMENT

I live in a world of loneliness
This is no source of comfort or solace
All my tools and strengths are depleted
I have no one to turn to

For all too long my love was my safe harbor
Now that is gone, and I am stripped bare
My ports in the storm have been devastated
My ship sails aimlessly in the winds of life

I feel totally alone
And no one can hear my plea
My voice calls out to the thunderous storm
And falls aimlessly on the rough seas

Is there a way out?
I cannot see it
I search in every direction
And all the doors are shut

What is there to do
I truly do not know
And feel that I will never find out

The sailor grows weary
Beaten down by the merciless sea

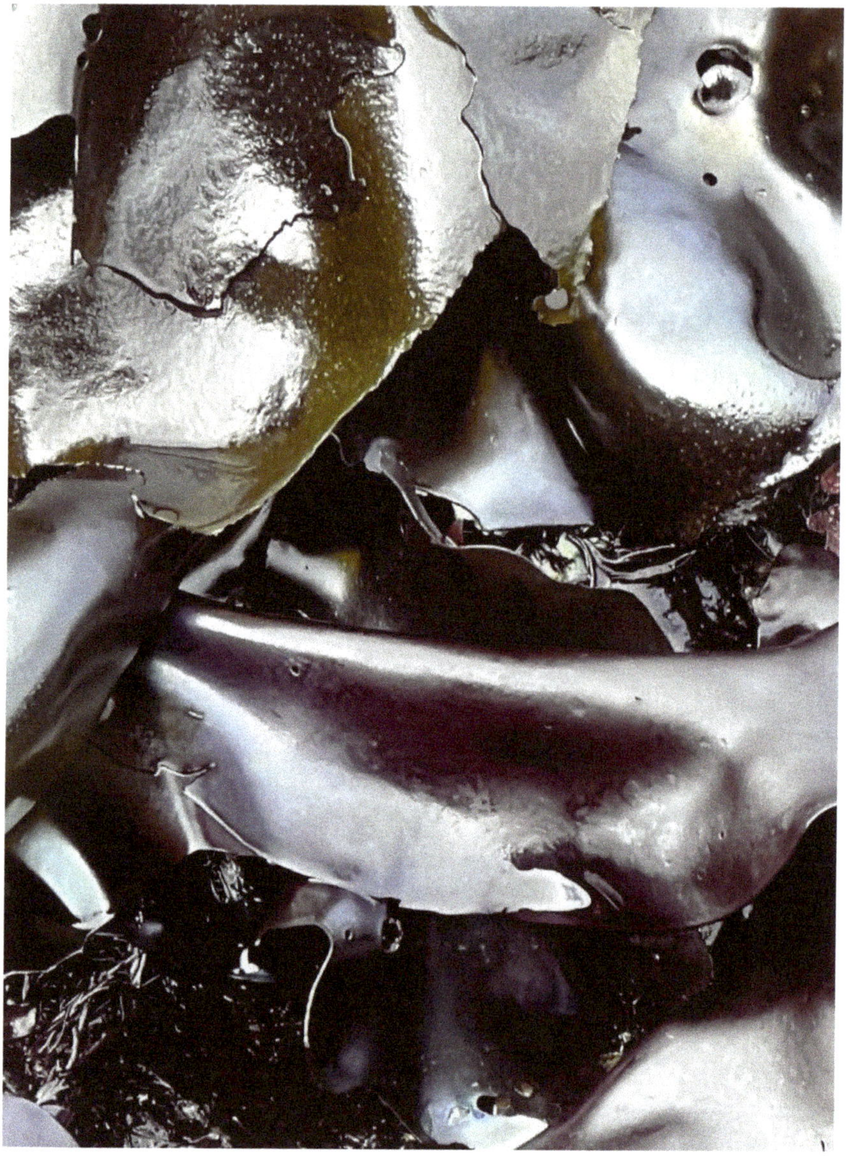

THE SCULPTOR

The snow falls softly from the grey streaked sky
It touches my cheek like the small sting of a needle
The wind bites into my being
I am alone on the vast beach

The early morning light is just beginning to illuminate the landscape
I see the tall dunes and watch the waving beach grass
Small objects, boats, flotsam and jetsam emerge from the grey as I approach
I walk briskly but with no special purpose

I am alone in a world that can be many things
It can be a world of interest, new discovery, and fascination
Or it can be a world void of humanity, a sphere of loneliness
It is what I am

I do not know how the sculptor will fasten the clay
I know it can form many objects but cannot yet see them
The clay starts to live
It takes on its shape and form-it lives

What is it to become
It grows with each moment
Beauty or beast
Joy or sorrow

All lies in the eye of the beholder

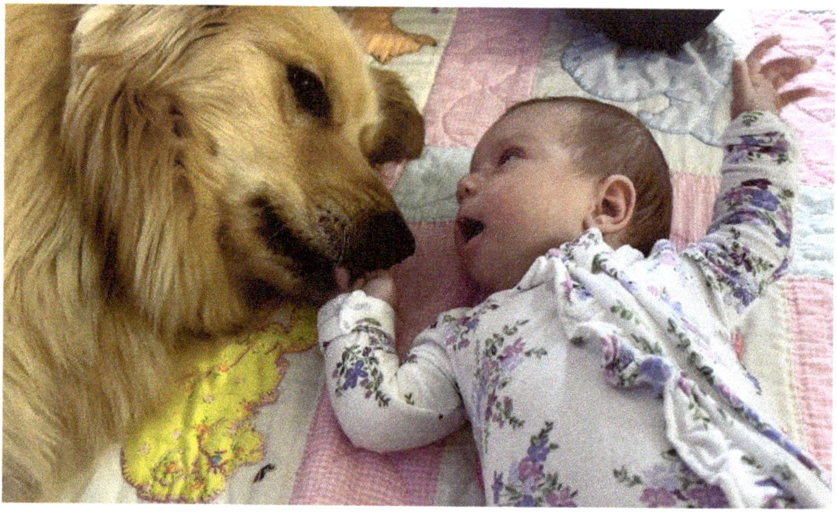

THE SOUNDS OF LOVE

As I walk through my world, I am bombarded by its sights and sounds
Some very pleasing and energizing and some a cacophony of sound and nonsense
Those that distract are painful to the ear and soul
And those that are pleasing add light and joy to a sometimes mundane existence

The sounds of my daughters' voices and those of their children
These are the true joys in my life
These are the sounds that can elevate the spirit
No matter how down I may be

These are the sounds that can make me smile
When all seems so sad
These are the sounds that add color, light, and laughter to my world
These are the sounds that nourish me and allow me to grow

These are the sounds of meaning, now and forever
Never let them grow silent

THE ULTIMATE BLOW

My world has been shattered into a thousand glass shards
Flying out and causing great damage to all within range
They seek to hurt and destroy
All that the years have created

And as they settle to the earth
The wounds are bandaged and the pain becomes less
Over time, there will be healing
Slowly, at first, and then more rapidly as the insult fades

I have done great damage and caused great pain
It was not done with purposeful intent
It was done so I could begin to breathe
For all the pain I have caused, I feel somewhat free

I have explicated the obvious and now must reconstruct my world

There will be times of great pain
And there will be times of great joy
The mix will be turned by the hands of time and fate
And the final amalgam will be my life

For better or for worse
This is my life

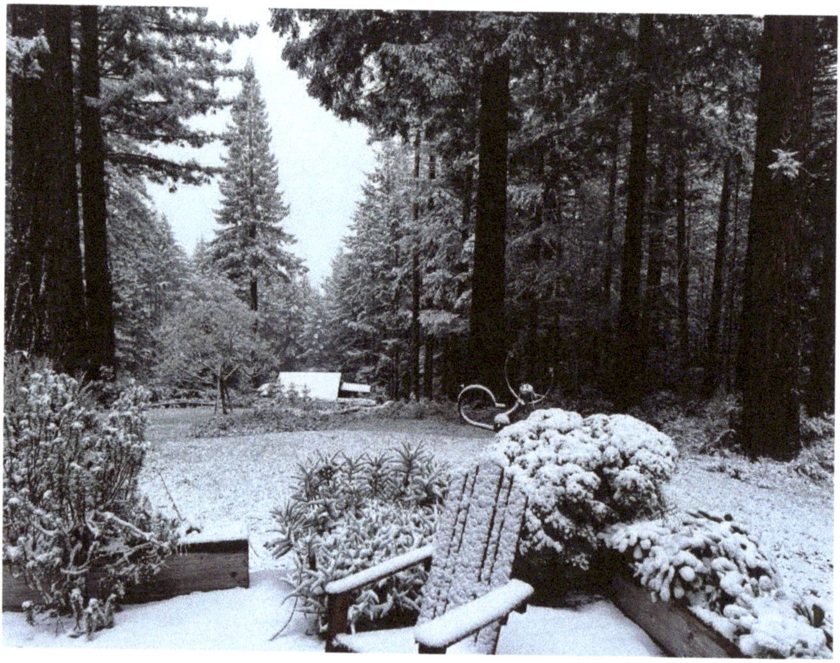

THE WINTER CHILL

Brother Sun, Sister Moon, see the beauty of the earth
See the snow sculptured trees and bushes
Feel the brisk tingle as the air lightly brushes your skin
Feel the hard crusted snow crunch under the weight of our step

Winter has come to our world
Once what was brown, green and red is now white and shimmering in the golden light
The dark shadows of the birds dance upon the white crusted snow
The wild turkeys prance and pluck, ever searching for food
We feel the sharp chill surrounding us at every turn

I walk through the world and my bones are cold
The wind cuts through our clothes like a sharp knife
And yet I am warmed by your presence
You take my arm and I feel a jolt of electricity
My body comes alive like a small fire has been kindled
We walk through the snowy landscape arm in arm
Laughing and jumping over the drifts like young puppies
Our love brings us warmth and comfort

The early light starts to disappear and darkness slowly falls
We are still far from the warmth of our home
So we hold each other tighter and run and ship over the frozen landscape

There is a small light off in the distance
It's glow beckons u and we charge forward
Soon we are at the door and we push it open and fall helter-skelter into the dark room
Only the light of our Christmas tree lights our space

I pull off my gloves and bend before the hearth
Quickly tearing paper, piling kindling and striking a match
The fire burst into the room throwing its light and warmth

We are warm and safe in our cozy room
We cuddle with each other stealing bits of heat from the other's body
We laugh and start at each cold touch from each other
And we revel in the warmth given by the other

We are two conjoined souls
Warmed and comforted by each other
We are alone and we are together. We are in love

THE WORDS OF LOVE

To have a meaningful relationship has certain rules and regulations
There should always be caring, kindness, consideration, and deep, unabiding love
And there should always be communication, the bridge that connects all

When one feels down, alone, isolated, or lost
The one thing that acts as a port in the storm
Is the kind word from a loving partner
It is the lifeline that can rescue, calm, and make right
All the badness, harshness, anxiety, and pain

It is those words that when delivered with love and caring
Make us safe, ground us, give us the support we feel we have lost
It is those words which can make us whole again, give us ground to stand on

Those are the words of love
And they should never be forgotten

Because when delivered
They make all right with the universe
They reconstruct our fragmented beings
Reassembling the broken parts
And make us live again

The words of love
The first thing you should hear in the morning and the last thing at night
They repair the damage of our lives
And they should never be forgotten

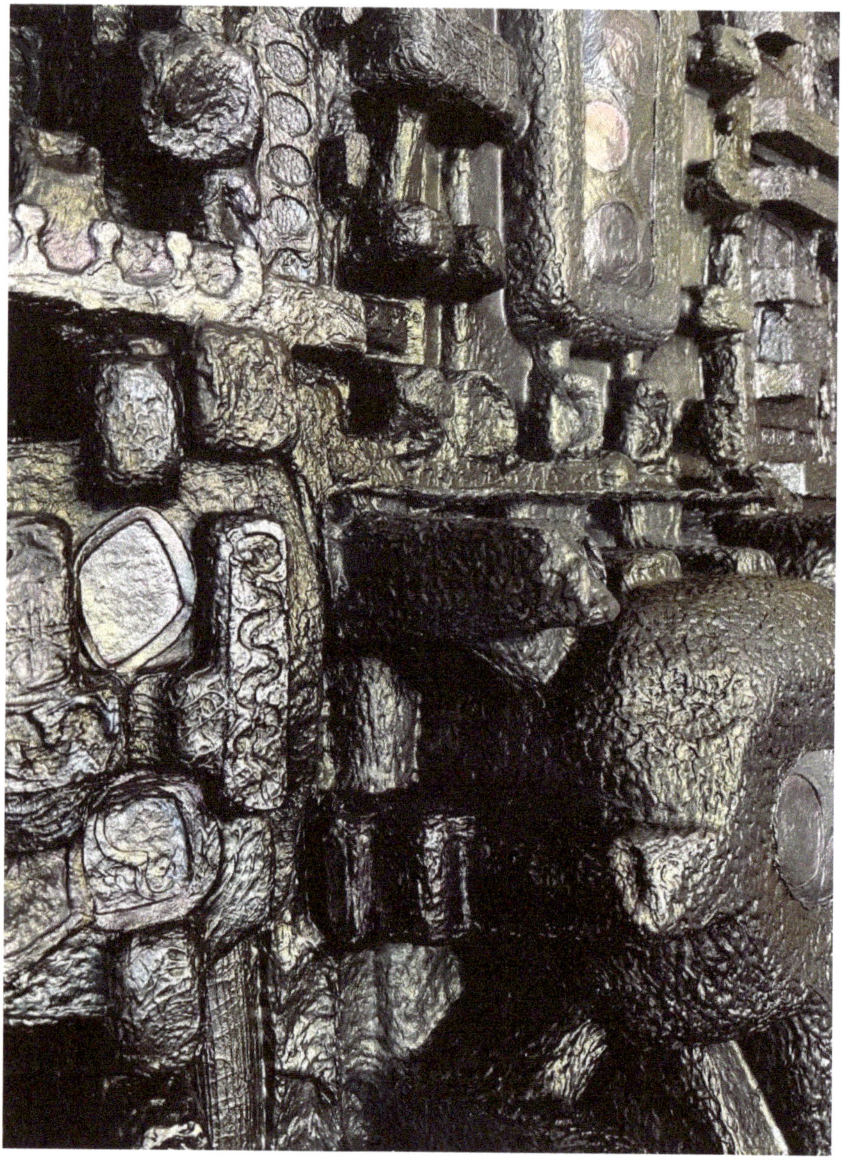

THE YAMMA-YAMMA MACHINE

The many thoughts race through my mind like the passing of freight trains
The clamor and confusion feels like I am lost in a train station
The noise and signs bombard my consciousness and I cannot find my way out
I am lost in the tumult of overwhelming, clouded, confusing information

My mind cannot find the peace it so strongly desires
It is buffeted by the thoughts, feelings, emotions, and fears which jumble together
To create a cacophony of confusion and helplessness
Looking very much like a tornado which can clearly be seen but not avoided

How to turn off the machinery
How to quiet the cacophony
How to find peace of mind
These are the tasks at hand
These are the tasks to be accomplished

I must learn the skill of prioritization
I must learn to separate things into parcels and put them in compartments
I cannot mix things that do not belong together
And I must learn to deal with what is before me rather than everything in the box

This task is not easy and requires constant vigilance
It is this vigilance which can be very wearing

It would be nice to turn off the YammaYamma machine
It would nice to fall into the solace of deep sleep
To dream again of things of fantasy
Of things that delight the mind
And not the things that torment it

I wonder how this can be done

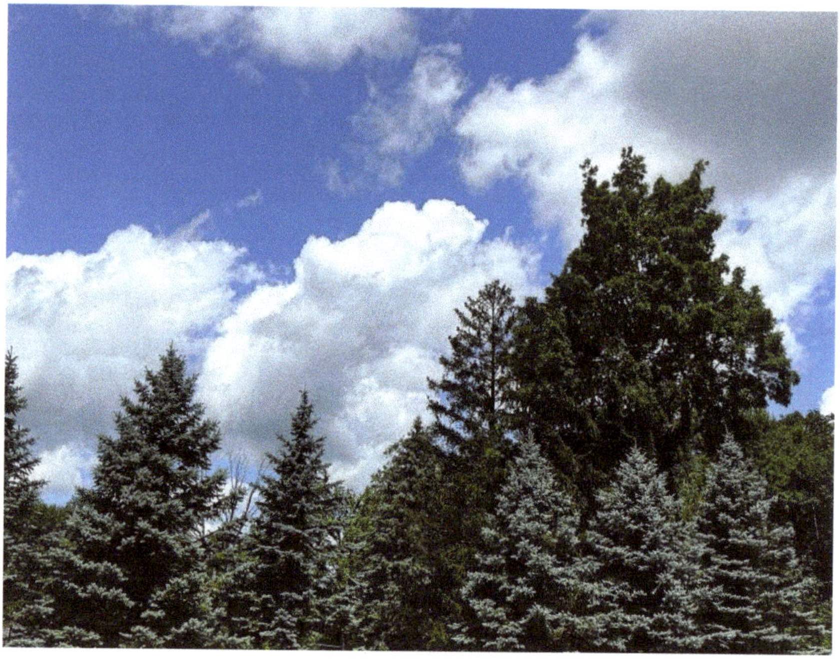

TODAY

The cool breeze blows across my exposed skin
It penetrates into the very depth of my bones
A shiver gently shakes my body

I see a little blue head peeking out of the snow
A crocus catches my eye and makes me think
Soon the season will change

Soon there will be light and warmth
The grey becomes blue and the brown becomes green
Only those with eyes can see this
Only those with a heart can feel it

I must be open to the changes

TORMENT

I lie down and sleep does not come
I pull the covers up, listen to the fan overhead
I hear my heart beating and I feel each breath come in and out
I toss and I turn
I cannot find sleep

My mind races on to my life or lack thereof
I see Deanne and the world of Lexington, and I feel lonely
I see my apartment and the hubbub of my neighborhood and I feel lonely

I go to my office to try to generate some meaningful work and I feel lonely
I go to the gym and lose myself in a spin class   I walk home, feeling lonely

Most times I just want to cry or jump out of my skin
I cannot find a place of solace
I am truly unhappy

What will become of me?
Will I live or die?
More importantly, will I ever be happy again?

I would love to smile
I would love to laugh
I would love to feel love again

And I wouldn't mind dying

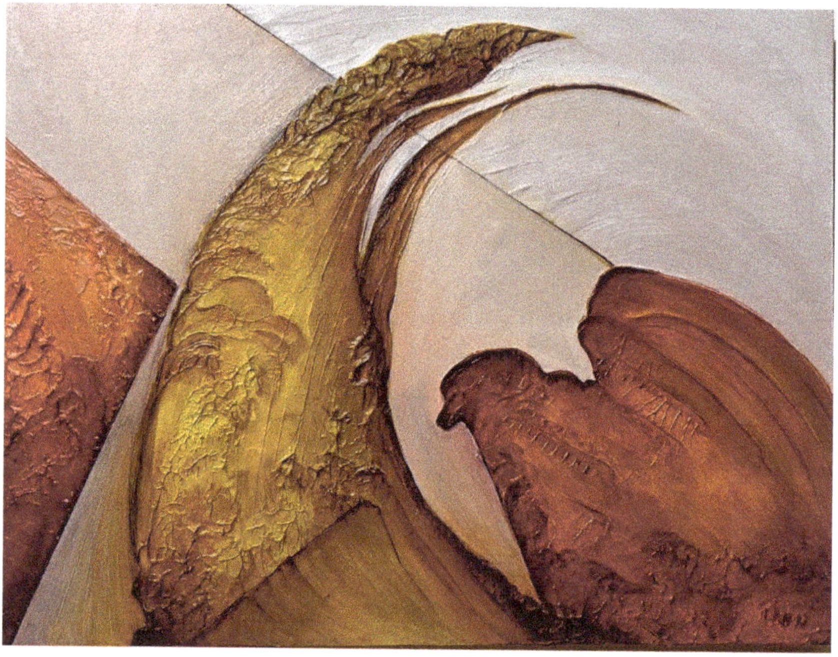

UNTITLED

The water trickles down, drip by drip, landing on my forehead
It never ceases, its cold splash slapping me awake
Not letting me rest
Not letting me take my mind elsewhere

I am trapped in the sand with only my head showing
It is cold and dark, and a cruel wind blows across my brow
I know that I cannot escape
I wait for the inevitable

I am so tired of waiting and wondering
I am no longer master of my own destiny
I am a ship in a storm which has no foreseeable end
I will eventually land but on which shore, I have no idea
The eventual end frightens me.

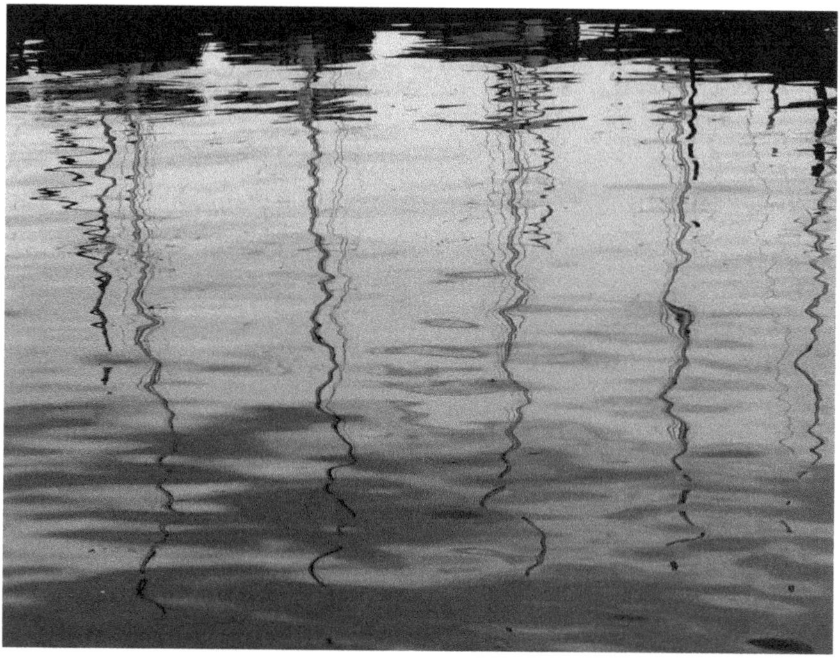

WHEN WILL I AWAKEN

The jarring jangle of the alarm clock brought me to reality
I was home, alone, and cold.
I got up, showered, brushed my teeth, and lay down to meditate

I managed to feel each breath and arose with a new outlook
My brief period of mindfulness serving as a reframer of life.

Off to the office where I could not keep focused
I think of you each minute
I see you in every image
I long for you

When will this period of abstinence end?
When can I begin to grow?
To come out of my doldrums?
To look anew at everything that I encounter?

I feel as if I am withering on the vine
Lacking nourishment and life-sustaining breath

I count the days, hours, minutes, and seconds
I can picture the future, but it is still too far to taste

The earth turns on its axis, yet it does not move fast enough
I must preserve my soul so that it is not too damaged

I so want to bring joy and energy to my life
To have my relationship serve as the gentle wind
That lifts my spirits and elevates to that higher plane
My mind, my body, my soul

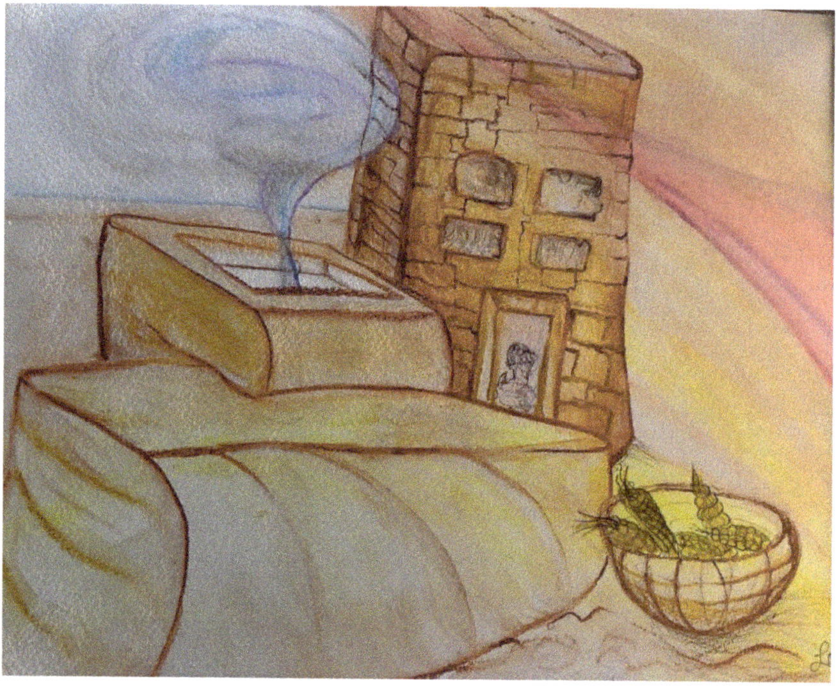

WHO WILL BE THE FIRST TO DIE

I sit alone in a world that I can no longer tolerate
All I have is distant and impossible to touch
My love has forsaken me
Left me alone to live or die
The choice is near impossible
And yet every day makes the decisions harder

I have given up
I cannot make this decision
I do not have the fortitude to move ahead
And thus I am left alone and unprotected.

It seems that the only choice is to make my exit
Who will grieve? I know there will be many
They will console each other, and life will go on
They will speak well of me
Probably better than I deserve

Is there a way out?
Right now, all the exits are blocked
There is no safe passage
My exit will help
My exit will….

WRITER'S CRAMP

I write to explore my feelings
Hoping to find the joy

It isn't working

The words try to open the shades
Letting in the light
Yet they are too hard to pull

No light gets in
The mind remains in darkness

A BIRTHDAY THOUGHT

The world is often very hard to walk
There are potholes and tough patches along the way
However, it is the path chosen
And it has many joys and wonders

I often wonder if some of the joys are not appreciated
They are there but somehow we miss them

Often the true joys and wonders must be searched for
Often hidden in dark clouds of insignificant discontent

I will continue to seek them out
Willing to take the extra steps necessary

I do this because I feel the work involved is certainly worth the reward
To walkaway from something that has given me such love and joy is foolhardy

To this path I will commit my efforts
Doing whatever work is necessary
And if I should falter
May my love reach down with a helpful hand
Or gentle encouragement

MY LOVE

The morning light creeps into my window
I turn and reach across the bed
I am alone
Something is missing

The warmth and love of companionship

It was there last night
As the light dimmed and faded
I could feel it in the warmth of a touch
In the gentleness of a kiss

It comforted me
Sleep overcame me

I drifted off
Into the Morpheus of another world

A BIRTHDAY THOUGHT

The world is often very hard to walk
There are potholes and tough patches along the way
However, it is the path chosen
And it has many joys and wonders

I often wonder if some of the joys are not appreciated
They are there but somehow we miss them

Often the true joys and wonder must be searched for
Often hidden in dark clouds of insignificant discontent

I will continue to seek them out
Willing to take the extra steps necessary

I do this because I feel the work involved is certainly worth the reward
To walk away from something that has given me such love and joy is foolhardy

To this path I will commit my efforts
Doing whatever work is necessary
And if I should falter
May my love reach down with a helpful hand
Or gentle encouragement

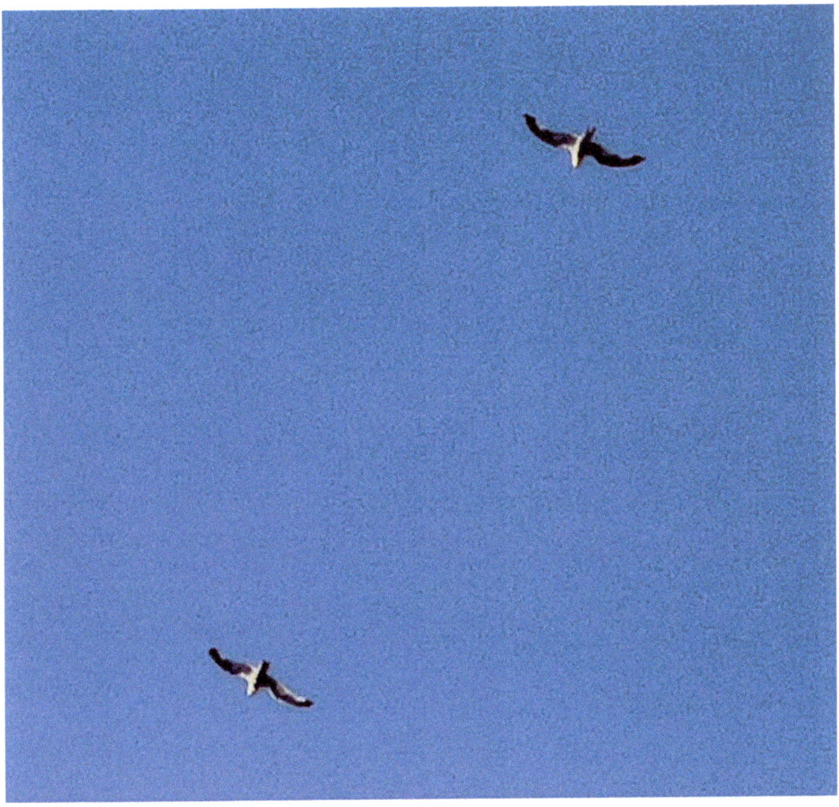

A LIFE WELL LIVED

The warm breeze rustles through the trees
The soft flapping of wings
Ducks landing on the pond
Soft effortless motion that places them
Ever so gently on the lily pada
The world seems alive and yet quiet
Celebrating the gift of being
Not disturbed just being

Into this drifts the memory
A life well lived
A life of joy, happiness and giving

A life of giving to family and friends
A life of giving to the many strangers
Who entered his sphere

A life of unbridled giving
To so many over such a short time

A LIFE WELL LIVED 2

We all grieve in different ways
And in our grieving, we must be thankful

To have been touched by the light
Which shown on us for the times we were given

We will pick up the pieces
And we will go on
So let us be thankful
For what we were given
And was not taken away

We are the better for the gift
Let us grasp our sorrow
Wringing from it all we now have
And why we are better
For that special gift
And why it forged who we are

Life gives
Life takes
We are human

FISHING

Up from the depths of the earth
Pushing a small pile in front of it

A creature moves ever so slowly
Inching its way across the green carpet

Stopping, slithering, stopping ever so slowly
I approach, measuring each silent step

Then in a flash – movement
The earthworm returns to the depths

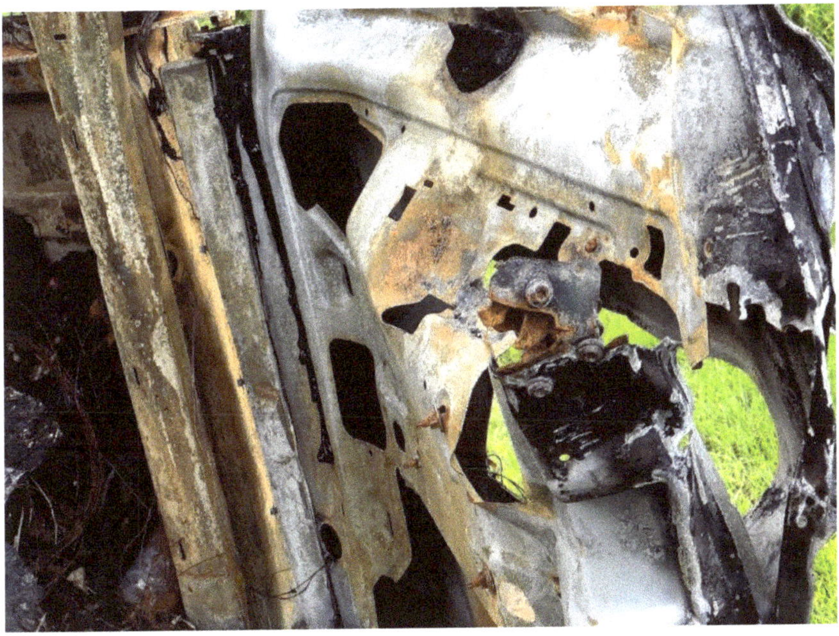

GALVESTON

The sun beats down on me as I walk the wide avenue
The humidity covers me like a blanket of moisture
And the light is as bright as a klieg

Houses dot the landscape as if scattered by the hand of a child
Some large, spacious, grand mansions, with a French flair
Then squalor, dilapidation, broken fences and barking guard dogs
A strange dichotomy, hard to justify or understand

What we see is the result of Mother Nature
A monster-killing storm rushed through, destroyed, and moved on
Leaving debris and destruction where once there was beauty and order

Now some restored to their previous glory, others left to weather and rot

We are watching evolution as it slowly moves through our daily light
It comes fast, changes us, and moves on like a shadow

LITTLE RED SCHOOLHOUSE

There was blood spattered across the room
Books, desks, walls, and children – left lifeless and limp
The destruction of bullets piercing wood, windows, and oh so young bodies
The tears, the terror, the unknown
The feeling of living in a horror novel

But yet so very real – so present
Will it ever stop
Only if we want to stop it

If not
More bodies, more stories, more guns, and so many more tears
More inaction

I THINK SO

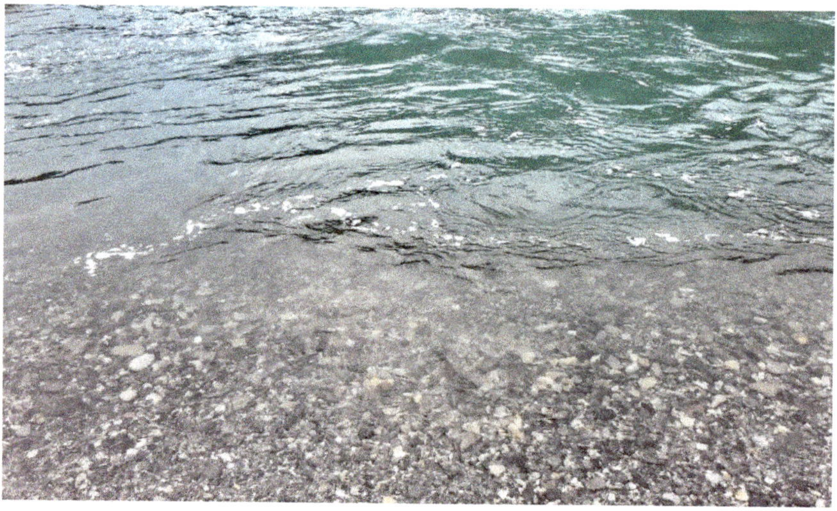

SUNDAY IN THE PARK

The gentle bubbling of the lazy brook
Runs through the wooded glen

A gentle rustling of the trees
Leaves floating to their resting place below

The stream is dancing with the colored accents
A small splash, an unusual sound

The frog leaps from stone to stone
Almost lifeless as it lands on the rock

A darting shade of brown
Leaps out from the creature

A small insect mysteriously disappears

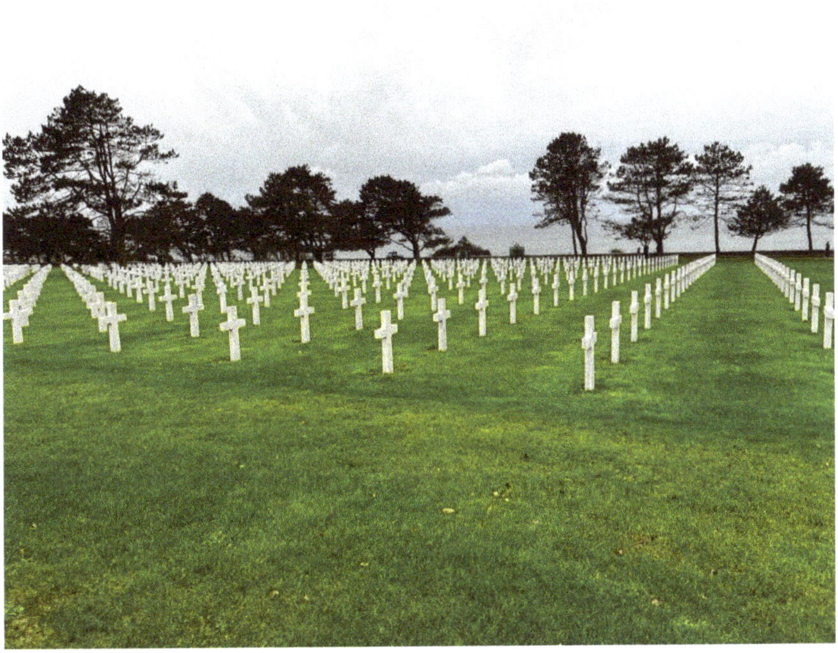

THE COLONEL

I walk the battlefield
Smoke, broken vehicles, bodies scattered everywhere
Broken and ghastly – mouths open, limbs lost, faces in agony

I walk among them
I wander hither and yon – no path is clear
A tear forms in my eye

These are my people
People I sent her to fight and die
The carnage is everywhere, I pull my scarf over my mouth

I wonder why
Is this my doing, was this necessary, DID I do this
I feel sick and take a drink from my canteen

I move back to HQ to check plans for my next encounter
I am the responsible party, and I think, I wonder

Can I continue
Of course I can – I am a tool of war

This is my life

THE HUNTER

As I look out my door there is a movement in the woods

I stand and I watch
The movement stops

I stand and I watch
A flicker of white
A young doe ventures forth
Still as a statue it looks in my direction
I dare not breathe, I dare not blink
I stand and watch

Shortly comes out – a frail small doe
The image of its mother
Creating a bucolic scene in the tableau of nature
They move ever so gently
I am transfixed by their grace and beauty

A twig snaps, ears go up – all is still
In an instant they are gone
The transient nature of the scene causes me to think

Grace and beauty are everywhere around us
We only need to see – with our hearts and minds

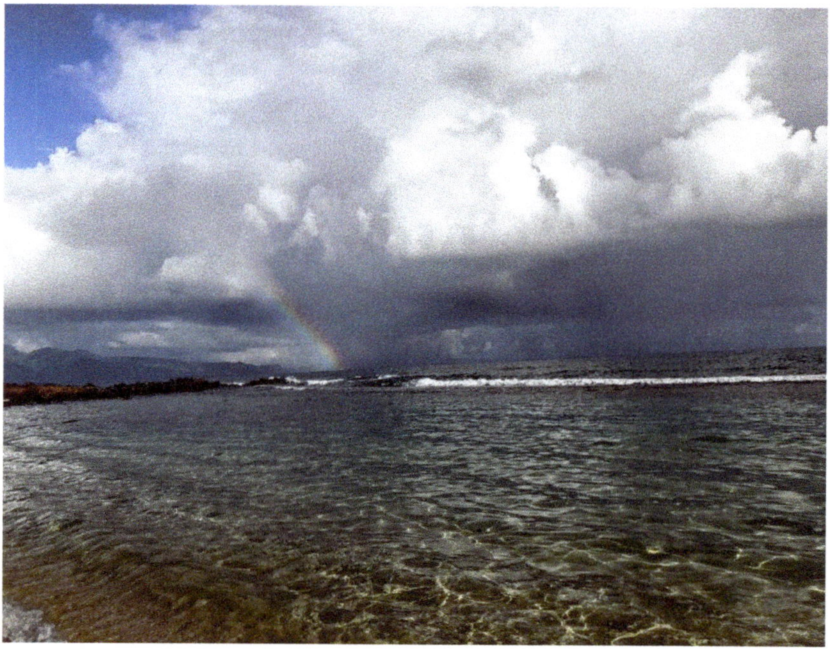

THE PASSING

It is fall

The brightly colored leaves drift on the downward breeze
I think of our loss

A friend is gone, and I am alone
Alone, without the joy of life and the daily celebration of joy

And then I ponder, the gift of his life
How it enriched all it touched
And how much its loss portends
For so many in so many ways\

I think of those left behind
To pick up the pieces which lie broken in our thoughts

And then I see the gift
Of the blessing that has been bestowed
On each and every one of us
A life well lived

THE POND

The yellow thrush warbled out its sweet song as the pond came to life
Tiny splashes at the edge of the water and the deep black mud signaled the presence of the frogs
And then all was quiet until the squirrel flew from the tree and landed on the mallow bush
And just as quickly scampered to safety, bringing quiet back to the pond

The quiet was broken by the rumble of a car traversing the dirt road above the pond
The crunch of the gravel and dirt alerted all to the approaching outsider into the quiet, private pond life
…and then the sound stopped again, momentarily, all was quiet

The slamming of two car doors and the joyous laughter of two young children came rushing forth

They run with great excitement to the edge of the pond and throw their lines out
Two splashes and children's happy chatter filled the air with a sense of wonderment
Hours passed, more chatter, and many more splashes, then a dash for the car
The quiet was broken once again by the sound of tires on gravel
All grew quiet. The usual pond sounds returned. The thrush sang his song

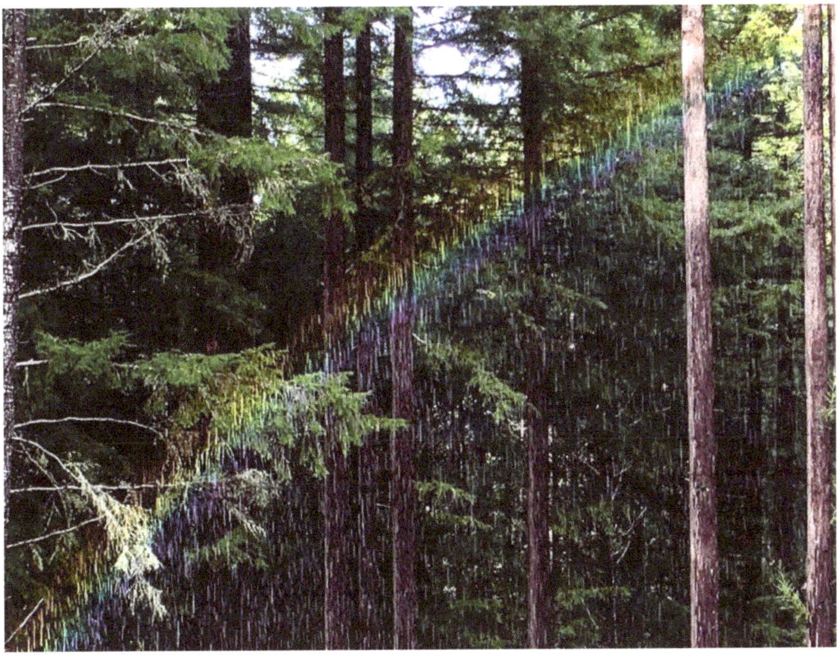

THE RAIN

I walk through the door
Colors and shapes bombard my senses
All is quiet

A gentle rain falls on the crisp grass
Little puddles form on the silvery stones

I pause, listen intently
I feel a gentle breeze

It blows over me like a silken cloth
All the world smells clean and crisp

The drops of water come more quickly
Soon I am just another, wiped clean by the rain

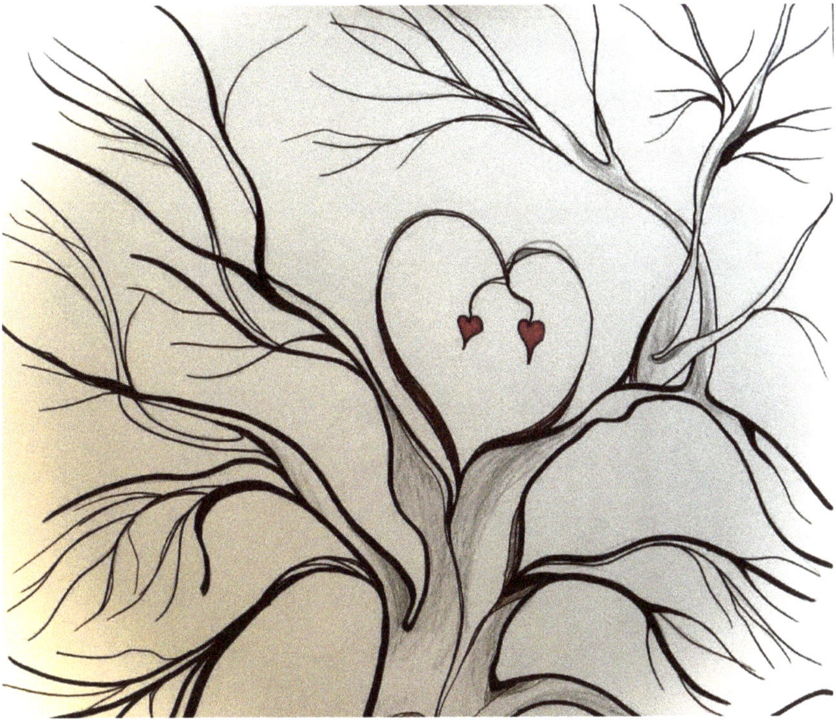

VALENTINES DAY 2024

The cold creeps into my being

I shudder and quiver, hoping to find comfort

Your face enters my room

I instantly warm and smile

A morning kiss is exchanged

I am warm and whole again

All is well-it is valentines day.

Printed in the USA
CPSIA information can be obtained
at www.ICGtesting.com
CBHW062240221124
17856CB00022B/803